THE ATLAS OF
WORLD
CULTURES

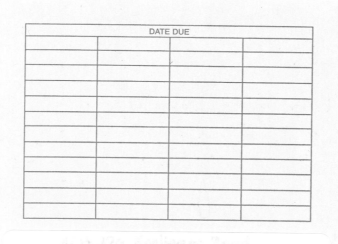

Published by
PETER BEDRICK BOOKS
2112 Broadway
New York, NY 10023

The Atlas of World Cultures was created and produced by
McRae Books
via de' Rustici, 5 Florence (Italy)

Text Brunetto Chiarelli and Anna Lisa Bebi
Main illustrations Paola Ravaglia
Other illustrations Alessandro Baldanzi, Alessandro Bartolozzi, Lorenzo Cecchi, Matteo
Chesi, Ferruccio Cucchiarini, Gianna Filetti, Antonella Pastorelli, Roberto Simoni
Translation Anne McRae
Graphic Design Marco Nardi
Color separations R.A.F., Florence (Italy)

Library of Congress Cataloging-in-Publication Data
Chiarelli, A.B.
The atlas of world cultures / Brunetto Chiarelli, Annalisa Bebi: illustrated by Paola Ravaglia.
p. cm.
Includes index.
Summary: Examines the people of the world and their unique cultures, religions, languages, geography and politics.
ISBN 0-87226-499-8
1. Ethnology—Juvenile literature. 2. Indigenous peoples—Juvenile literature. 3. Manners and customs—Juvenile literature.
[1. Ethnology. 2. Indigenous peoples. 3. Manners and customs.]
I. Bebi, Annalisa. II. Ravaglia, Paola, ill. III. Title.
GN333.C55 1997
306—dc21   96-52309
CIP
AC

Printed in Italy

01   02   03   1   2   3   4

THE ATLAS OF WORLD CULTURES

Dr. Brunetto Chiarelli
and Anna Lisa Bebi

Illustrations Paola Ravaglia

Alessandro Baldanzi, Alessandro Bartolozzi
Lorenzo Cecchi, Matteo Chesi, Ferruccio Cucchiarini
Gianna Filetti, Antonella Pastorelli, Roberto Simoni

PETER BEDRICK BOOKS
NEW YORK

Contents

THE HUMAN STORY

Human evolution
According to the theory of evolution, apes and humans share a common ancestor. About 4 million years ago, human ancestors had evolved the main skeletal features – changes in the hips and feet enabling them to walk upright, increased brain size, and modified jaw – that distinguish them from the apes. These hominids are called australopithecines (southern apes). They lived in Africa between 4 and 1.7 million years ago. *Homo habilis* (*Homo* = man, *habilis* = handy) is the earliest being that scientists call human. *Homo habilis* was able to use tools. *Homo erectus*, who made use of tools and fire, dates from about 1.5 million years ago. Modern humans (*Homo sapiens sapiens*) developed about 100,000 years ago in Africa and spread throughout the world. The map below shows the dates modern humans are believed to have reached various parts of the world.

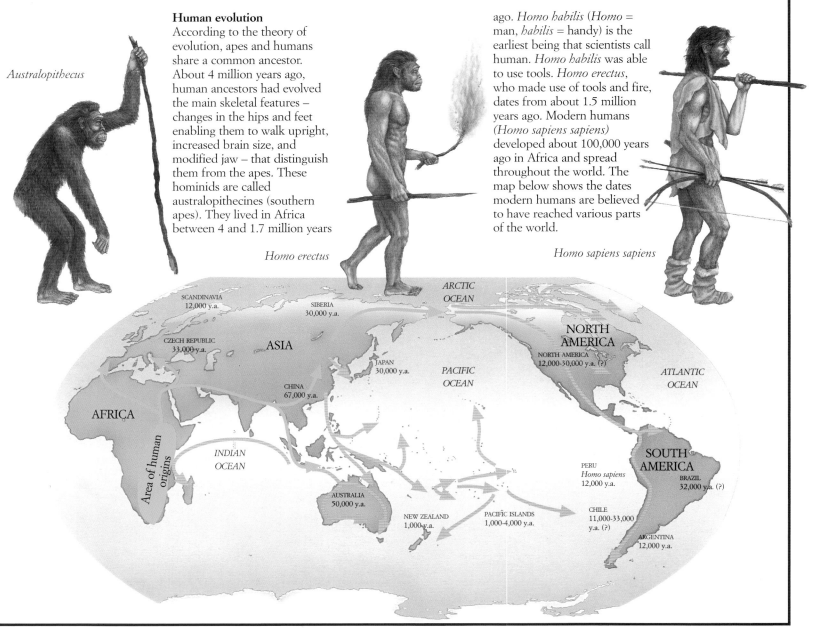

Australopithecus

Homo erectus

Homo sapiens sapiens

SCANDINAVIA 12,000 y.a.

SIBERIA 30,000 y.a.

ARCTIC OCEAN

CZECH REPUBLIC 33,000 y.a.

ASIA

NORTH AMERICA

NORTH AMERICA 12,000-30,000 y.a. (?)

JAPAN 30,000 y.a.

PACIFIC OCEAN

ATLANTIC OCEAN

CHINA 67,000 y.a.

AFRICA

Area of human origins

INDIAN OCEAN

SOUTH AMERICA

PERU *Homo sapiens* 12,000 y.a.

BRAZIL 32,000 y.a. (?)

AUSTRALIA 50,000 y.a.

CHILE 11,000-33,000 y.a. (?)

NEW ZEALAND 1,000 y.a.

PACIFIC ISLANDS 1,000-4,000 y.a.

ARGENTINA 12,000 y.a.

Scientific research in the developed world seeks cures for disease.

Introduction

There are more than 6 billion people in the world today. We are all members of the same human family that developed in Africa and spread across the globe. This book sets out to explore the ways in which we live, our beliefs, languages, religions, art, clothing, housing, families – in short, our cultures and social organization. The most striking thing about people and human societies is how greatly we differ and how varied human culture is. There are peoples today, such as the nomadic Tuaregs in the Saharan Desert, who continue much as their ancestors did thousands of years ago, while other people live in modern apartments in huge cities. They are connected by phone, television, and the internet to millions of other people on other continents. We will also look at some of the problems in the world today like hunger and conflict, and the clash of interests that often occur between people of the Western world and traditional peoples.

World population is growing rapidly.

In traditional societies older people are honored and respected for their knowledge and experience.

Many refugees and people displaced by natural disaster and famine have no place to live.

Two worlds
Wealth is not distributed evenly throughout the world. Some countries, such as Canada, the US, Japan, Australia and New Zealand, Great Britain, and many countries in Europe, are rich. They are referred to as "developed" or "industrialized". Other countries, mainly in Africa, Asia, and Latin America are poorer, and are called "developing" nations.

Families
The family is the basic social unit in almost every human society. Families differ greatly around the world. They can consist of any number or combination of people, from just a single parent and child, to large groups of people related by birth or marriage.

Conflict
Conflict and war have been present in human societies since prehistoric times. One long-term effect of war is that it creates refugees. There are about 20 million refugees in the world today. This is too large a number of people to resettle in other countries. Many refugees live in camps for years at a time.

Many people still get their water from open wells.

Education
School is compulsory for all children in the developed world and almost everybody learns to read and write. In the developing world, fewer children attend school and literacy rates are lower.

Throughout the developing world fewer girls than boys are allowed to attend school. This is a serious problem in our overpopulated world, since it has been shown that the more education a woman receives the fewer children she is likely to have.

Water
One in five people in the world today do not have access to safe drinking water. Over 25,000 people die each day from illnesses they catch from drinking unclean water. Most unsafe water is in the developing world. It is caused by untreated sewage being discharged into rivers and lakes. In the developed world, unsafe water is caused mainly by industrial wastes.

World population today

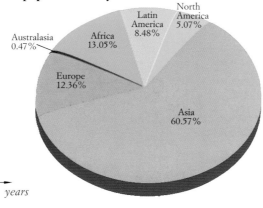

Region	%
Australasia	0.47%
Africa	13.05%
Latin America	8.48%
North America	5.07%
Europe	12.36%
Asia	60.57%

Population growth 1750-2025

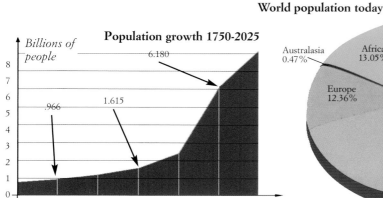

Billions of people
- 6.180
- 1.615
- .966

years: 1750, 1800, 1850, 1900, 1950, 2000, 2025

Percentage of city-dwellers by continent

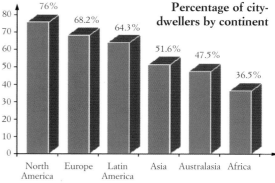

Continent	%
North America	76%
Europe	68.2%
Latin America	64.3%
Asia	51.6%
Australasia	47.5%
Africa	36.5%

Population growth
The population of the world is growing very quickly. It took one million years to reach a global population of one billion. Today it will take only 10 years to add a further one billion people. Population is growing more quickly in the developing world than in industrialized countries. Central and Southern Africa have the highest growth rates in the world. The countries of Western Europe have the lowest growth rates.

Where people live
Asia is the largest continent in the world. It is also the most populous. Almost two-thirds of the population of the world now lives in Asia. Many parts of Asia, including India, Bangladesh, China, and Japan, are among the most densely populated areas of the world. Western Europe is also a densely populated region.

Urbanization
At the beginning of the 21st century, almost two-thirds of the population of the world now lives in towns and cities. This is a huge increase on previous figures. The number of city-dwellers has doubled in the last 40 years. Towns and cities will continue to grow this century. Most of the largest cities will be in Latin America, Asia, and Africa. Cities in some areas are joining together to form megalopolises. In Japan, for example, Tokyo, Osaka, and Kyoto nearly touch.

Northern Europe

Northern Europe is composed of the British Isles, Scandinavia, and Iceland. It has been invaded many times over the centuries, and is now inhabited mainly by peoples of Germanic origin. In the Viking age (800–1050 AD), the Scandinavians, who were superb sailors, traded with, raided, and settled many other countries, including the British Isles. The Vikings were the first Europeans to reach America, about 500 years before Columbus. Much later, from the 16th century onward, people from the British Isles also settled in distant countries. They went to live in the Americas, Australia, New Zealand, Africa, and Asia; everywhere that had become a part of the British Empire. In this way the English language and British culture and ideas spread around the globe.

The countries of the British Isles and Scandinavia today are all wealthy, modern democracies. The majority of people live and work in cities. English is the most widely-spoken language in the British Isles. In Scandinavia, the Danes, Swedes, and Norwegians speak closely related Nordic languages. In Finland, both Swedish and Finnish are spoken.

Iceland
Iceland was settled in the 9th century by Vikings from Norway. Icelanders still speak a language that is related to Norwegian. Many work in the fishing industry. Lutheranism is the main religion.

A multicultural society
When the British Empire broke up in the 20th century, some people from the former colonies chose to live in Britain. Many came from the West Indies and the Indian Subcontinent. Their traditions have changed and enriched British culture.

Scotland
Traditionally, the people of Scotland are divided between the Celtic Highlanders and the Anglo-Saxon Lowlanders. Although the Scots and Gaelic languages persist, English is now spoken by almost everyone.

Shaggy Highland cattle at an agricultural show.

In some rural areas daily life continues much as it has for centuries.

Irish troubles
Ireland was divided in two in 1920. Since the 1960s Northern Ireland has been torn by outbreaks of extreme violence between some Roman Catholics who want to join the Republic of Ireland and Protestant groups who do not.

Celtic brooch from Tara, home of the first Irish kings.

Irish writers
Ireland has given English literature some of its finest writers, including Jonathan Swift, George Bernard Shaw, William Butler Yeats, Oscar Wilde, James Joyce, and Samuel Beckett.

The Commonwealth and the EU
Britain still heads the Commonwealth, an association of independent states formerly part of the British Empire. It is also a member of the European Union.

Unemployment
Unemployment is a problem not only in the British Isles, but throughout Western Europe. It is particularly serious when young people are without jobs. They sometimes lose hope and become involved in drugs and crime.

Celtic languages
The British Isles were inhabited by Celts until the Anglo-Saxons invaded in the 4th-6th centuries and pushed them into the western and northern fringes of the Isles. Pockets of Celtic languages have survived in Scotland, Ireland, and Wales to this day.

Sports in the British Isles
Cricket and rugby are sports traditionally associated with the British Isles. Tennis and golf are also widely played. However, as in many other parts of the world, soccer is probably the most popular spectator sport today.

The United Kingdom and Ireland
England, Scotland, Wales, and Northern Ireland are known as the United Kingdom. All four countries are ruled from the parliament at Westminster, in London. The Republic of Ireland is a separate country and is governed from its own parliament in Dublin.

British Islands
Most of the Channel Islands and the Isle of Man are part of Britain.

Blacksmith shoes a horse on the island of Jersey in the Channel Islands.

Fisherman from the Faroe Islands, in the North Atlantic. The islands are a part of Denmark.

The Saami

The Saami people, or Lapps, as they are also known, live in Norway, Sweden, Finland, and Russia. They have lived here for at least 2,000 years. The Saami language is related to Finnish, but not to the other Nordic languages. Today there are about 65,000 Saami speakers. Only a few thousand live traditional lives as nomadic reindeer herders or hunters and fishermen.

Saami woman. Each Saami group has its own traditional colors and dress.

Scandinavians and the sea

In Scandinavia the sea has always been an efficient means of travel and a source of food. Fishing was once the basis of daily life for many people. Today, the fishing industry is big business.

The sport of cross-country skiing began in Scandinavia.

The origins of Skiing

Skiing originated in the snow-covered Nordic countries as a means of travel and transport. Skis dating from almost 5,000 years ago have been found in the bogs of Finland and Sweden. Skiing is still used for transport in some areas, but is primarily a winter sport.

Forestry worker in Finland.

The Icelandic sagas

The story of the settlement of Iceland by Norwegian Vikings is recorded in the 12th-century Icelandic sagas. They also tell of Viking voyages of discovery in the North Atlantic, including Leif the Red's journey to America. They provide a unique glimpse into the lives and beliefs of people in medieval Scandinavia.

Religion in Scandinavia

Christianity was introduced to the region in the 9th century. Nowadays, the Protestant Lutheran Church is the most widespread. It is based on the teachings of Martin Luther, and spread to Scandinavia in the 16th century.

Medieval wooden stave church, in Norway.

Bronze ornament from the prow of a Viking warship.

St Edward's crown, used in the English coronation ceremony.

Tall, pointed houses typical of the historical parts of Nordic cities.

Forestry

Finland, Norway, and Sweden are heavily wooded. The lumber industry plays an important role in their economies.

Monarchies

Denmark, Great Britain, Norway, and Sweden are all monarchies. This means that they have a reigning king or queen. Even so, they are all governed by freely elected parliaments. The monarch is a figurehead or symbol for the people of each country.

Life in Scandinavia

The four Scandinavian countries enjoy very high living standards. They have excellent education, health, and welfare systems. English is the main second language throughout this region, where most people speak at least two languages.

NORWAY
Pop. 4,400,000
Cap. Oslo

SWEDEN
Pop. 8,900,000
Cap. Stockholm

FINLAND
Pop. 5,100,000
Cap. Helsinki

DENMARK
Pop. 5,260,000
Cap. Copenhagen

ICELAND
Pop. 300,000
Cap. Reykjavik

UNITED KINGDOM
Pop. 58,900,000
Cap. London

IRELAND
Pop. 3,600,000
Cap. Dublin

The Breton language

A Celtic language, called Breton, is still spoken in some parts of Brittany. Related to the Celtic languages of Great Britain, it spread to Brittany in the 4th-6th centuries when Anglo-Saxon invasions caused some English refugees to flee to France.

NETHERLANDS
Pop. 15,700,000
Cap. Amsterdam

BELGIUM
Pop. 10,200,000
Cap. Brussels

LUXEMBOURG
Pop. 406,000
Cap. Luxembourg

FRANCE
Pop. 58,600,000
Cap. Paris

MONACO
Pop. 32,000
Cap. Monaco

Women in Brittany wear traditional costume, including tall lace caps, during annual Roman Catholic pilgrimages, called pardons.

Tourism

France has a rich history and millions of tourists visit its museums and historic places each year.

Many foreign students study at the famous Sorbonne University in Paris.

Paris

Paris (sometimes called "the City of Light") was founded over 2,000 years ago on a small island in the river Seine. Modern Paris now covers nearly 900 square miles and has over 9 million inhabitants. It is one of the largest cities in Europe. Paris is a world center of business, commerce, education, entertainment, food, the arts, and fashion. Central Paris is divided in two. The *rive gauche* (left bank) is the seat of intellectual life, while the *rive droite* is the economic center of the city.

The Pyramid in the courtyard of the Louvre Museum, is just one of many modern architectural monuments built among the beautiful historic buildings of Paris.

Church built by the influential French architect Le Corbusier.

Religion in France

The majority of French people are Roman Catholics, although only a small minority attend mass regularly. There are about 1 million Protestants of various sects, and about as many Jewish people.

The Loire Valley

The Loire is the longest river in France. The Middle Loire Valley was once the center of a rich agricultural area and a seat of the French court. Today the many historic châteaux (castles) and elegant parks recall its glorious past.

The Château Azay-le-Rideau

Cultural life

Paris was the center of cultural life in the Western World for most of the 20th century. Writers and artists poured into Paris from all over Europe (and North America). Concerts, theater, movies, art galleries, and museums continue to attract millions of visitors each year.

Lascaux

Lascaux cave in southwestern France is decorated with engraved, drawn, and painted animals, dating from about 15,000 years ago. Early inhabitants probably used the cave for magical hunting rites.

Life in the country

Only about 25 percent of French people now live in the country, and only a small minority work on farms. However, French agriculture is highly mechanized and agricultural products form an important part of French export items.

Provence traditional cape.

Language

French is a Latin language. Like Spanish, Portuguese, Italian, and Romanian, it is derived from the Latin which was spoken throughout the Roman Empire. Other languages spoken in France include the Occitan (or *Langue d'oc*) dialects of the southeast. Occitan had a rich literature during the Middle Ages. Up until the French Revolution in 1789 it was the main language in this area.

French farmer during the grape harvest. France is probably more famous for its wines than any other country in the world.

Because of the number of people of North African origin in France, the Islamic faith is now the second religion, after Roman Catholicism. There are more than 400 mosques in France.

Immigration in France

France has always had a substantial immigrant community. Up until the 1980s most immigrants came from neighboring European countries, such as Italy, Spain, Belgium, and Poland. Nowadays, most immigrants come from ex-colonies in North Africa. Racial intolerance, encouraged by extreme right-wing political groups such as the National Front, has increased in recent years.

Fine food

The French are united by their love of good food and wine. French cuisine varies greatly from region to region. For example, olive oil and garlic are as typical of Provence in the south, as butter, cream and apples are of Normandy in the north.

Cosmopolitan Amsterdam

Amsterdam celebrated its 700th birthday in 1975. Its historic center, built around a network of canals, is an important seat of business and commerce. About 12 percent of the population is foreign-born. Many come from Holland's ex-colonies in Indonesia and Suriname. The city has a long tradition of being open-minded and tolerant.

Amsterdam is a popular destination for young people from all over the world.

In many parts of Holland people dress up in traditional costumes to attract tourists. This woman is from Marken, just north of Amsterdam.

Reclaimed from the sea

Almost a fifth of the land in Holland has been reclaimed from the sea. The new land is fertile and makes excellent farmland. Dutch farmers raise cattle, for meat, butter, and cheese, and grow fruits, vegetables, and flowers for the home and export markets.

Horticulture is a highly technical business.

Dutch and Flemish painters

Over the centuries Holland and Belgium have produced many important painters, including Rembrandt, Bosch, Rubens, Van Eyck, and Van Gogh.

Detail from an early work by Vincent van Gogh, portrays Dutch peasants eating potatoes.

European Union

The European Economic Community, formed in the late 1950s, sought to improve trading conditions within Europe. It was very successful. The Community, now referred to as the European Union, will introduce a single currency and banking system throughout Europe. The various governing bodies of the European Union meet in Strasbourg (France), Brussels, and Luxembourg.

Benelux

The word Benelux refers to Belgium, the Netherlands, and Luxembourg. It is formed by combining the first letters of the names of the three countries.

Divided Belgium

Belgium is divided between French-speaking Walloons in the south, and Dutch-speaking Flemings in the north. Situated in the middle of the country, the capital city of Brussels is bilingual. There is also a German-speaking minority in the east. All three languages are official.

Flemish flag.

Buildings in the elegant Grand Place, *the central square in Brussels.*

Hergé created Tintin *and his dog* Snowy *in 1930.*

A museum of comics

Writers and illustrators from Belgium and France have created some of the best-loved comics around the world. *Astérix*, a comic strip about the invincible Gauls of France who resisted the Romans, was created by French writer René Goscinny and illustrator Albert Uderzo. Hergé (Georges Rémi), a Belgian, created another famous character, called *Tintin*. The works of Hergé and many other Belgian illustrators are displayed in the Comic Museum in Brussels.

Corsica

The Mediterranean island of Corsica has been a part of France since 1769. French is the official language, although the Corsican dialect is closer to the Italian spoken in Tuscany. Many Corsicans feel that they are not French and would like to be independent of France.

Tourism and agriculture are the main economic activities in Corsica.

France and Benelux

France and Benelux (Belgium, the Netherlands, and Luxembourg) were originally settled by successive waves of Germanic and Celtic peoples from Central and Eastern Europe. France and southern Belgium were occupied by the Romans for 500 years during the Roman Empire (27BC – 476AD). During that time they adopted the Latin tongue of their conquerors, which gradually evolved into modern French. In the north, the Franks, a Germanic people, repulsed the Romans and took control. They are the ancestors of today's Dutch-speaking inhabitants of Holland and northern Belgium. Both France and the Netherlands had many overseas colonies during the 17th to 20th centuries. Today both countries have large immigrant populations from their former colonies. Tiny, independent Luxembourg and Monaco are among the smallest states in Europe. Like Holland and Belgium, they both have reigning monarchies. France has been a republic since the French Revolution in 1789 which overthrew the royal family. It is one of the leading industrial powers in the world today.

Beguines – a female lay order

The Beguines are a sisterhood of women who live religious lives but who have not taken vows. The order originated in Holland in the 12th century and still exists in Belgium and Holland today.

Central Europe

Central Europe was settled by Celtic peoples in the 5th century BC. The area has been invaded many times, but the most significant invasions were those of the Germanic and Slav peoples in the 4th-6th centuries AD. The Slavs settled in present-day Poland and the Czech and Slovak Republics, and the Germans moved into modern Germany, Austria, and Switzerland. The languages spoken today still reflect this basic division. German is the predominant language in Germany, Austria, and Switzerland, while Slavic languages are spoken in Poland and the Czech and Slovak Republics. World War II left Germany in ruins. It was split into two countries – East and West Germany. The West quickly rebuilt its industry and economy. Since the late 1950s West Germany, Switzerland, and Austria have enjoyed strong economic growth and high standards of living. Immigrants, called "guestworkers", from Southern Europe and Turkey flooded into West Germany when labor was required. Many settled there with their families. At the end of World War II, East Germany, Poland, and Czechoslovakia lived under the Soviet communist regime. All three became independent of the Soviet Union in 1989. East Germany was reunited with its Western half in 1990. Poland and the Czech and Slovak Republics now have freely-elected governments.

POLAND
Pop. 38,700,000
Cap. Warsaw

CZECH REPUBLIC
Pop. 10,300,000
Cap. Prague

SLOVAK REPUBLIC
Pop. 5,400,000
Cap. Bratislava

AUSTRIA
Pop. 8,100,000
Cap. Vienna

GERMANY
Pop. 81,800,000
Cap. Berlin

LIECHTENSTEIN
Pop. 31,000
Cap. Vaduz

SWITZERLAND
Pop. 7,200,000
Cap. Bern

The Protestant Church
Protestantism began in Germany in the early 16th century. It spread from there to the rest of Europe and, gradually, all over the world. Germans today are divided between Protestantism (mainly in the north), and Roman Catholicism (mainly in the south).

The new Germany
Since the 1970s many Germans have tried new or 'alternative' lifestyles. Germans also travel widely. Most now take one or two holidays abroad each year.

In many parts of Germany beautiful half-timbered houses have survived from the Middle Ages.

Miner from the Ruhr valley.

Even in modern Central Europe, centuries-old traditions and customs linger. Feasts and holidays are often celebrated in traditional dress, with folk dancing, music, and food.

German economic power
Germany is a highly industrialized nation. It is Europe's leading economic power. Many people are employed in industries, such as mining, car-making, ship-building, chemicals, and high technology.

Neuschwanstein Castle was built at the end of the 19th century by Bavarian King Louis II, known as "Mad Ludwig". Louis was a fan and supporter of composer Richard Wagner. Each room in the castle is dedicated to one of his compositions.

Life in the mountains
The Alps, the tallest mountains in Europe, run through the middle of Switzerland and Austria. Winter sports, such as skiing, attract tourists from all over Europe.

Multilingual Switzerland
Switzerland is divided into 23 provinces, called cantons, each with its own traditions. The main languages spoken are German, French, and Italian. Most people speak more than one language.

In Switzerland scary wooden masks are hung outside houses during Carnival. They are meant to scare evil spirits away.

Fisherman packing up his nets at night.

The northern coast
Both Germany and Poland border the Baltic Sea, and Germany also faces the North Sea. Legends abound of pirates, such as Klaus Störtebecker, who once terrorized the area. Today there are bustling ports, such as Hamburg in Germany and Danzig in Poland.

Poland
Tragic events took place in Poland in the 1940s. During the Nazi occupation in World War II, over six million people were exterminated by the Germans. Most were Jewish people, gypsies, and those who opposed the Nazi regime.

German girl in traditional costume in the Czech Republic.

The Brandenburg Gate in Berlin. They city was also divided in two, from 1961-1989.

Catholic procession with the Madonna through the streets of Warsaw.

United Germany
Divided into two separate countries for 41 years, on October 3, 1990, East and West Germany were reunited.

The Catholic Church in Poland
Despite over 40 years under the anti-religious Soviet regime, Poland has remained strongly Roman Catholic. Over 90 percent of the people are still devout Catholics.

Minority groups in Central Europe
Small minority groups exist in all the countries of Central Europe. Because of this tension sometimes develops, as it has in Slovakia where ethnic Hungarians are asking for independence. Conflict has also arisen in Germany, where Turkish and other immigrants have sometimes been the victims of extreme episodes of racist violence.

Café life in Prague
The artists and writers of Prague used to meet in the *kavarni* (cafés). One of the most famous was the Café Argo, where the famous writer Franz Kafka often went to meet his friends.

Wine is produced, and enjoyed, throughout Central Europe.

Czech and Slovak Republics
In 1993 Czechoslovakia split into two separate states. The Czech Republic is larger and has more industry than Slovakia. Its Czech-speaking people have traditionally been linked to Austria and Western Europe. The Slovakians, who speak their own Slovak language, have stronger ties with Hungary and the Balkans in the south.

Oktoberfest
A great many traditional feasts and historical events are celebrated in Germany. Wine festivals, beer festivals, and hunting and harvest festivals are just a few of the common ones. The *Oktoberfest* held in Munich each year is one of the most well-known beer festivals.

A special beer is brewed each year for Oktoberfest.

Bohemia
The historical region of Bohemia is now a part of the Czech Republic. It has been famous for its beautiful glassware since the 13th century.

Violinist at the annual Salzburg Festival in Austria held in honor of Mozart at his birthplace.

Glass-making today in Bohemia.

Dairy farming and cheese-making are still important activities in the alpine areas of Switzerland and Austria today.

The earliest inhabitants
Human ancestors arrived in Europe about 700,000 years ago. Much later, modern humans came from Africa. This female figure, found at Willendorf, dates to 25,000 BC. It may represent a fertility goddess or the "Earth Mother".

Classical music
Many of the greatest composers of classical music, including Bach, Mozart, Beethoven, and Wagner were born in Central Europe. The Berlin Philharmonic and the Vienna Philharmonic are just two of the many famous orchestras today.

Austria
The people of Austria speak German. The majority are Roman Catholics. Like many developed countries in Europe, natural population growth is almost zero. Any increase in population is now caused by immigration.

Southern Europe

The Iberian peninsula and Italy were populated by modern humans from Africa about 30,000 years ago. Much later, Indo-Europeans from the steppes north of the Black Sea migrated into the area. Almost all the languages of modern Europe are descended from their tongues. About 2,000 years ago, Italy was the center of the Roman Empire, which united the Iberian and Italian peninsulas politically and culturally. The Roman Empire was destroyed by invasions of Germanic peoples. Muslim Arabs invaded and occupied parts of Spain from the 8th to 13th centuries.

SPAIN
Pop. 39,400,000
Cap. Madrid

SAN MARINO
Pop. 25,000
Cap. San Marino

PORTUGAL
Pop. 9,900,000
Cap. Lisbon

ANDORRA
Pop. 68,000
Cap. Andorra-la-Vella

ITALY
Pop. 57,100,000
Cap. Rome

VATICAN CITY STATE
Pop. 1,000
Cap. Vatican City

MALTA
Pop. 366,000
Cap. Valletta

Fishing
Fish are an important part of the Mediterranean diet. The famous fish and rice dish called *paella* comes from Spain. Fishing is one of the main industries in Portugal.

Gypsy girl dancing the flamenco.

Gypsies
Gypsies came to Europe from India in about 950 AD. The gypsies of Andalusia, called Flamencos, gave their name to the music and dance called *flamenco*.

The Basques
The Euskaldunak people, better known as the Basques, have lived in northeastern Spain and southeastern France for centuries. The Basque language is unrelated to the other languages of Europe. Linguists believe that it dates from before the arrival of the Indo-Europeans, making the Basques are one of the oldest peoples in the region.

Making port wine in Portugal.

Artists
Some of the greatest modern artists are of Spanish origin. Pablo Picasso, Joan Miró, Salvador Dalí, and Antonio Gaudí, for example, were all born in Spain.

The Church of the Holy Family, in Barcelona, by Gaudí.

Holy Week in Spain
The week before Easter is a time of special celebration, especially in the south of Spain. Long processions of penitents carrying crosses, and floats with Madonnas, pass through towns and villages to the Cathedral. Many penitents wear tall, pointed hats called *capuchones*.

Wine making
Italy, Spain, and Portugal are among the leading wine-producers in the world. Wine has been produced in these countries for centuries. The Ancient Romans planted vines wherever they settled and wine was widely drunk. During the Middle Ages wine-making traditions were kept alive by monks in their monasteries. Nowadays wine from these countries is exported all over the world.

Girl in traditional costume on the island of Ibiza.

Arab influence
From the 8th to 13th centuries Arabs reigned over much of Spain. Traces of their presence can still be found in buildings, traditions, and language.

Al Qal a al-Hambra, or the Red Fort, built by the Arabs at Granada in the 13th century.

The Balearic Islands
The Balearic Islands have been inhabited for at least 6,000 years. Nowadays they are a favorite spot for tourists.

Language in Spain
Castilian, or modern standard Spanish, is spoken throughout Spain. Other widely spoken languages are Catalan, Galician, and Basque.

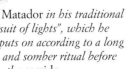
A Matador in his traditional "suit of lights", which he puts on according to a long and somber ritual before the corrida.

Sports
Bullfighting, *la corrida de toros* in Spanish, is one of the most popular sports in Spain. Bullfighters, called *matadores*, risk their lives in the arena every Sunday afternoon during the season, which lasts from March to October. In recent years other sports, such as soccer, have also become very popular.

Immigration
The gap between the wealthy countries on the northern shores of the Mediterranean and the poorer African nations to the south, has caused an upsurge in migration from Africa into Europe. An increasing number of Africans, alone or with their families, are leaving their homelands in search of work in Europe. Many immigrants have also come from Eastern Europe.

Spain, Portugal, and Italy played central roles in the development of modern Europe. The Renaissance in Italy in the 14th to16th centuries revived scholarship in literature, science, and the arts. Spain and Portugal were prominent players in the Age of Exploration, founding overseas empires that stretched from the Americas to the Philippines. In the 20th century, all three countries lived under fascist dictatorships, although they are all now modern democracies. The official languages in the three countries are based on Latin and are quite closely related. Catholicism is the predominant religion.

Italian fashion
Italian fashion and design are famous around the globe. Each season buyers and celebrities from around the world gather about the catwalks of Milan, Florence, and Rome for a preview of next year's fashions.

Italian traditions
Nearly every Italian village or town celebrates its patron saint or re-enacts a famous event, by dressing up in costume, preparing special food, and often, playing traditional games. In Siena, for instance, the *Palio* horse race around the central piazza takes place twice each summer. In Florence, neighborhood teams meet for a game of *calcio in costume,* an early form of rugby.

Carnival in Venice
Most people in Southern Europe are Roman Catholics. They celebrate Carnival, which is the period of feasting and fun before the austere 40 days of Lent, leading up to Easter. The celebrations in Venice are particularly striking. The carless, canaled streets of central Venice enter a time warp, as the city fills with people in fancy dress and masks from other ages.

Moving north
Southern Italy and the islands have always been poorer and less developed than the industrialized North. Since the fifties, many Southerners have settled in the large northern cities of Milan, Turin, and Genoa, where they can find work.

Medieval costume in Tuscany.

Italy – a kaleidoscope of languages
Italian is the main language in Italy. But many other languages are spoken as well. In the the South, there are communities of Greek-, Albanian-, Croat-, and Catalan-speakers. In the northern border areas, there are German, French, and Slovenian minority groups. There are also many different languages spoken by recent immigrants.

Rome
The ancient city of Rome was once the center of the Roman Empire. It is now the capital city of Italy, and home to the Vatican State, where the Pope and the Roman Catholic Church are based.

St. Peter's Cathedral, in Rome.

Woman of Albanian descent in southern Italy.

Sardinian shepherd.

Sardinians
Traditionally, the people of Sardinia were shepherds. The island's extensive rolling pastureland is ideal for sheep farming. Recently, tourism and industry have also become important.

Sicily
The largest and most populous of the Mediterranean islands, Sicily has always been a crossroads of culture. Greeks, Phoenicians, Vandals, Ostrogoths, Arabs, Normans, and Byzantines are just some of the peoples who have left their mark on the island.

Remains of a Greek temple in Sicily.

Malta
The islands of Malta are inhabited by people of Arab, English, and Italian origin. English and Maltese are the official languages. Malta was settled very early and traces of its first inhabitants are among the oldest in the Mediterranean basin.

Prehistoric female figure, from Malta.

Zero population growth
Italy has one of the lowest population growth rates in the world. The number of children born is dropping each year, and zero population has almost been achieved.

On the great Hungarian Plain, or puszta, *skilled horsemen called* Csikosok *breed and train spirited horses.*

Hot springs in Hungary
The Ancient Romans were the first to use public thermal baths to improve health. Today, there are more than 150 hot-spring baths in Hungary. They are used by Hungarians and tourists alike.

Romanian shepherd.

A Hungarian man relaxes under a tanning lamp at a thermal bathhouse.

The Hungarians
Most Hungarians are part of an ethnic group called Magyars who immigrated from Eastern Europe in the 9th century. They speak Hungarian, a language which is related to Finnish and Estonian.

An elderly Croat woman prays using rosary beads.

The Mostar Bridge
The beautiful Mostar Bridge, destroyed in the recent civil war, has become a symbol of the brutal conflict in ex-Yugoslavia.

Romania
Like other Balkan countries, Romania developed a modern economy based on industry and services under communist rule. About half the population live in cities.

New Balkan states
After the peace settlements in 1996, the newly independent states of ex-Yugoslavia were established along ethnic and religious lines.

Bulgaria
Bulgarians speak a language of Slavic origin and are mainly Eastern Orthodox in religion.

Bulgaria produces most of the rose-oil used (to make perfume) throughout the world.

Eastern Orthodox church in Albania.

Albania
Albanians are descendants of the ancient Illyrians. They have lived in the region for at least 3,000 years. They are mainly Muslim, although some follow the Greek Orthodox and Catholic religions.

Albanian woman in traditional costume.

The Greek Orthodox Church
The Greek Orthodox Church is one of the main branches of Eastern Orthodoxy. Most people in modern Greece still follow the Orthodox faith.

Greek Orthodox priests have long hair and beards.

A Macedonian woman offers walnuts from her garden to a United Nations peacekeeping soldier.

Greece
Modern Greeks are bound together by a common religion, a single language, and a great past. Greece is a full member of the EU. It has a developed economy and low birth-rates. Tourism is important for the Greek economy.

Conflict in the Balkans
The end of communist rule in Albania, Bulgaria, Romania, and Yugoslavia in 1989-90, brought rapid change. While the first three countries are on the way to becoming modern democracies, Yugoslavia dissolved into civil war as various ethnic groups fought for independence.

A Greek fisherman examines his catch in the beautiful Greek islands.

KEBEPOZ

The Balkans and Turkey

HUNGARY
Pop. 10,200,000
Cap. Budapest

ROMANIA
Pop. 22,600,000
Cap. Bucharest

BULGARIA
Pop. 8,760,000
Cap. Sofia

SLOVENIA
Pop. 2,000,000
Cap. Ljubljana

CROATIA
Pop. 4,490,000
Cap. Zagreb

BOSNIA-
HERZEGOVINA
Pop. 4,480,000
Cap. Sarajevo

SERBIA
Pop. 10,540,000
Cap. Belgrade

ALBANIA
Pop. 3,440,000
Cap. Tirana

TURKEY
Pop. 63,700,000
Cap. Ankara

CYPRUS (Greece / Turkey)
Pop. 750,000
Cap. Nicosia

MACEDONIA
Pop. 2,200,000
Cap. Skopje

GREECE
Pop. 10,450,000
Cap. Athens

The countries of southeastern Europe are called the Balkans, from a Turkish word meaning "mountains". They are joined on their southern tip with the huge country of Turkey, which straddles the continents of Europe and Asia. Many great civilizations have flourished here. The most famous of these was Ancient Greece. Even today, Western governmental systems, science, art, and literature bear traces of Greek thought. The Byzantine Empire, based in Constantinople, was another great power. It lasted 1,000 years, until the 15th century, when the Ottoman Turks destroyed it. The Ottomans controlled the Balkans until the 19th century. They introduced the Islamic religion, which is still practiced in many countries. The Ottoman Empire survived in Turkey until early in the 20th century. In recent years the Balkans have been shaken by ethnic struggles, communist rule, and brutal civil war. Turkey and most of the Balkan states now have democratic governments. Throughout history this area has been a crossroads for peoples of vastly different origin. This heritage is reflected in the mix of cultures, languages, and religious creeds that thrive today.

Gypsies
There are many Gypsies in Romania and Bulgaria. This man is part of the Kalderash group.

Karagöz shadow theater
A traditional form of Turkish entertainment, the theater is named after its main character, Karagöz. Karagöz theater developed in Turkey and then spread to Greece and North Africa.

Istanbul
Overlooking the Bosphorus, which separates Europe from Asia, the city of Istanbul (previously Constantinople) has seen much of European history pass beneath its walls.

Turkish shepherd relaxes near his flock.

Turkish wrestlers in action.

Wrestling – a national sport
Wrestling is popular in Turkey. Once practiced in country villages and nomadic camps, it is now done in modern gyms. It is called *yagli* in Turkish, which means oil, because the wrestlers grease themselves all over before they start.

The peoples of Turkey
Turkey has been a melting pot of different ethnic groups and cultures since prehistoric times. In modern Turkey most people speak Turkish, although there are small minorities of Kurdish and Arabic-speakers. Islam is the dominant religion.

The bronze horse and rider of Artemision; a striking work of Greek art.

Cyprus
The Mediterranean island of Cyprus has changed hands many times through the centuries. Since 1974 it has been spilt into two separate parts, one Greek and one Turkish. Cypriots speak either Greek or Turkish, depending on where they live. Most people make a living from tourism or agriculture.

An artisan in Cyprus prepares traditional metal work, now mainly sold to tourists.

Art and sport in Ancient Greece
Ancient Greece was one of the most important and well-known of the great civilizations of the past. It was famous not only for its poets, philosophers, and art, but also for its athletes. The Olympic Games were invented here to celebrate their sporting prowess.

Eastern Europe

Eastern Europe consists of the countries of the former Soviet Union as far east as the Ural Mountains. Slav peoples have lived here since about the 5th century AD. The area was invaded many times by, among others, the Vikings (who were probably the first to call it "Rus"), and the Mongols under Genghis Khan. The Grand Princes of Moscow gradually freed Russia and surrounding lands from the Mongols. One Grand Prince, Ivan the Terrible, was crowned Tsar of all Russia. Over the following centuries the Tsars conquered most of Eastern Europe, Central Asia, and Siberia. They continued to reign until 1917 when they were toppled by the Bolshevik revolution, and the Soviet Union was established. Under the communist regime all private property, including land and industry, was transferred to the state. Many people disagreed with these policies and they were often enforced by violence. After World War II the Soviet government extended its influence over many countries in Eastern and Central Europe. From that time the world was polarized between the United States and the Soviet Union in what was called the "Cold War". After 1985 a new Soviet leader, Mikhail Gorbachev, introduced processes called *glasnost* (openness), *perestroika* (reconstruction), and *demokratizatsiya* (democratization). This led to the collapse of communism. By the early 1990s the Soviet Union had splintered into several independent republics. The heartland, now called the Russian Federation, is faced with serious economic and political problems, and is struggling to become a modern democratic country.

The Baltic States
The Baltic States comprise the countries of Lithuania, Latvia, and Estonia on the Baltic Sea. All three gained their independence from the Soviet Union in 1991. Under Soviet rule, large numbers of Russians immigrated into the Baltic States. Most have remained. Religion (Lutheranism in Estonia and Latvia, and Catholicism in Lithuania), and folk culture have all blossomed since independence.

RUSSIA
Pop. 148,000,000 (including Siberia)
Cap. Moscow

ESTONIA
Pop. 1,600,000
Cap. Tallinn

LATVIA
Pop. 2,600,000
Cap. Riga

LITHUANIA
Pop. 3,800,000
Cap. Vilnius

BELORUSSIA
Pop. 10,200,000
Cap. Minsk

UKRAINE
Pop. 51,700,000
Cap. Kiev

MOLDAVIA
Pop. 4,500,000
Cap. Kishinev

GEORGIA
Pop. 5,600,000
Cap. Tbilisi

ARMENIA
Pop. 3,700,000
Cap. Yerevan

AZERBAIJAN
Pop. 7,500,000
Cap. Baku

Nenets – people of the Arctic
The Nenets live in the tundra of the far north, near the Urals. Once nomadic reindeer herders, they followed the animals north in the summer and south again in winter. Last century many were forced to settle. The men continue to herd reindeer, but most of the women stay with their children in villages.

Nenet family wearing a mixture of traditional clothing made from reindeer hides and modern garments.

Farming
Russia has large areas of fertile farmland. Under Soviet rule all farms were state owned. While investment in industry was great, agriculture was neglected. Farm machinery was hard to get and of poor quality. Land is now being returned to private owners, but they still don't have the machinery, fertilizers, and knowledge to bring Russian farming up to European standards.

Horse-drawn carts and plows are a common sight in many parts of Russia.

Space exploration
The Soviet Union was active in space exploration. During the 1950s and 1960s it achieved a number of firsts in the space race, including the launch of the first satellite, the first man to orbit the earth (Yuri Gagarin), and the first woman in space (Valentina Tereshkova). More recently, Russian scientists have concentrated on living in space. The orbiting space station *Mir* has been inhabited by people for up to seven months at a time.

Russian astronaut on his return from Mir space station.

Cultural life
Russian literature, music, and art have played a central role in European culture. Composer Tchaikovsky, novelists Tolstoy and Dostoyevsky, and dramatist Chekov, are just some of the most famous names. Today, movies are the most popular form of entertainment.

Ballet is an art at which Russians have always excelled. The Bolshoi and other dance theaters are famous throughout the world.

Estonian woman during a traditional festival to celebrate the return of spring.

Jews in Russia
Since *perestroika* the Jewish religion is once again practiced openly, although anti-semitism is still a problem. It has forced more than one million Jews to emigrate since 1960.

Getting away from it all in Russia means having a dacha (a house in the country).

Cleaning up the environment

The drive to improve industry under communism was harmful to the environment. Toxic wastes pumped directly into the air, earth, and water have led to health problems in many areas.

Economic hardship

The change from a centrally planned economy to a free market has not been easy. Soaring food prices have caused hardship for many people.

The Russian Orthodox Church

Russian Orthodoxy is a form of Christianity. It was founded by Prince Vladamir I of Kiev in 998. Under Soviet rule all religions were strongly discouraged. Since the late 1980s this has changed. There has been an upsurge in religions of all types, including Russian Orthodoxy, Islam, Roman Catholicism, Lutheranism, the Baptist Church, Judaism, and Buddhism.

Icons showing sacred people or events are important in teaching the Orthodox religion.

Caucasus – struggling for independence

The Caucasus Mountains, covering an area about the size of California, are home to at least 50 different ethnic groups. When the Soviet Union collapsed, Azerbaijan, Georgia, and Armenia proclaimed independence. Other groups, like the Chechens, would also like to be free of Russia. War broke out in Chechnya in 1994, but Russia refuses to give up the area. Other groups are also at war, including Christian Georgia and Muslim Azerbaijan, as they fight it out for control of a pocket of land.

A woman in Chechnya reacts to losing her house after Russian bombing.

Oil in the Caspian Sea

The Caspian is the world's largest inland sea. It is important for transport in the area. It also has rich oil and natural gas deposits, which is why Russia is so reluctant to grant independence to all the states along its coast.

Many of the oil rigs in the Caspian Sea are produced in Azerbaijan.

Caviar

The city of Astrakhan at the mouth of the Volga River on the Caspian Sea is the capital of Russian caviar. The roe (eggs) of the sturgeon fish is carefully removed. It is considered a great delicacy all over the world.

Many Russian Jews choose to emigrate to Israel. In 1990 alone, 400,000 Russians moved to Israel.

Corn is used to make mamalyga, a kind of porridge. It is the national dish of Moldavia.

Moldavia and the Ukraine

The rich farm land in these countries was developed under the Soviet regime. They were called the bread basket of the Soviet Union. Cereals, vegetables, and fruit are the main crops. There are over 100 different ethnic groups in the two countries, including Ukrainians, Moldavians, Russians, Poles, Bulgarians, Tartars, Armenians, Gypsies, Kazakhs, and Jews.

A country babushka (grandmother) and her granddaughter face the future together.

Mother Russia

Rodina, or the "motherland", is the European heartland of Russia, home to the East Slav people for centuries. They speak Russian, which is written using the Cyrillic alphabet. This part of Russia and Siberia are now called the Russian Federation. It is the largest country in the world.

Ancient beliefs have mingled with Christianity and Islam in the Caucasus. In some areas every house in a village had a corresponding one in a neighboring "village of the dead". When people died they were laid to rest in the replica of their house.

Folk group in Georgia doing a rain dance. Since Georgia has one of the highest yearly rainfall figures in Eastern Europe, it appears to be working!

Language and Writing

In traditional Aboriginal societies, elders pass on their culture by telling stories.

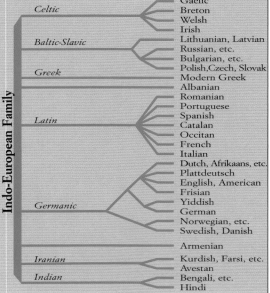

In international sign language this sign means "come back".

People use language to exchange information, or communicate. Human language consists mainly of speech, and also of writing. Speech existed many thousands of years before writing was invented. We don't know exactly when (or where, or how, or even why), people began to speak. But we do know that our ability to use language so efficiently is one of the reasons why we have been able to create complex societies. People have an innate ability for speech. This means that children don't need to be taught to speak, they learn naturally from those around them. Written language is different because reading and writing have to be learned.

Oral languages
Some languages have never been written down. They pass from generation to generation by word of mouth, or "orally".

Sign languages
Many deaf-mute people use sign languages to talk. These involve gestures and hand signs, and sometimes lip-reading.

LANGUAGES OF THE WORLD

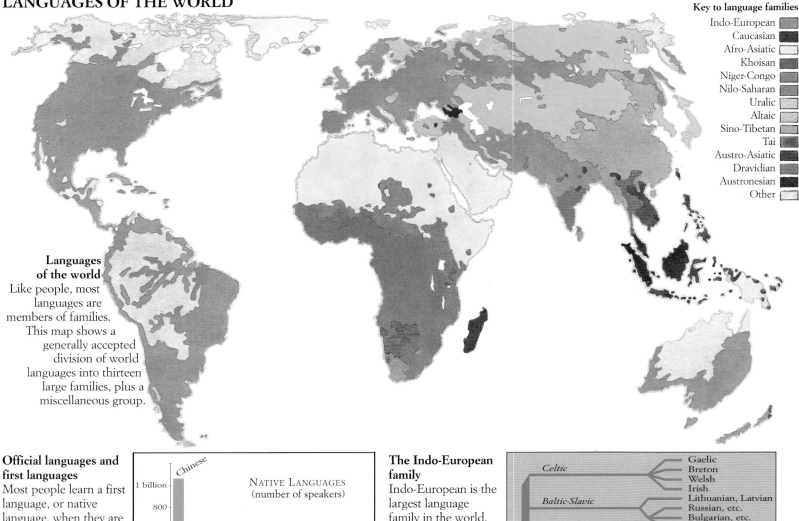

Key to language families

- Indo-European
- Caucasian
- Afro-Asiatic
- Khoisan
- Niger-Congo
- Nilo-Saharan
- Uralic
- Altaic
- Sino-Tibetan
- Tai
- Austro-Asiatic
- Dravidian
- Austronesian
- Other

Languages of the world
Like people, most languages are members of families. This map shows a generally accepted division of world languages into thirteen large families, plus a miscellaneous group.

Official languages and first languages
Most people learn a first language, or native language, when they are children. Many people learn to speak more than one language and are called "bilingual" if they speak two languages and "multilingual" if they speak more than two. In countries where a number of languages are spoken, one or more are chosen as "official" languages and are used in schools, on T.V., and by the government.

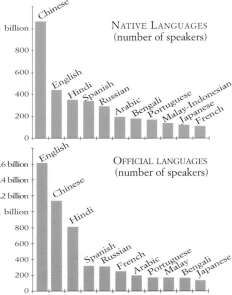

NATIVE LANGUAGES (number of speakers)
- Chinese — 1 billion
- English
- Hindi
- Spanish
- Russian
- Arabic
- Bengali
- Portuguese
- Malay-Indonesian
- Japanese
- French

OFFICIAL LANGUAGES (number of speakers)
- English — 1.6 billion
- Chinese
- Hindi
- Spanish
- Russian
- French
- Arabic
- Portuguese
- Malay
- Bengali
- Japanese

The Indo-European family
Indo-European is the largest language family in the world. It includes most of the languages of Europe, including English, French, German, Portuguese, and Spanish. Many of these languages have spread to other parts of the world and are now spoken by millions of people.

Indo-European Family

- **Celtic**
  - Gaelic
  - Breton
  - Welsh
  - Irish
- **Baltic-Slavic**
  - Lithuanian, Latvian
  - Russian, etc.
  - Bulgarian, etc.
  - Polish, Czech, Slovak
- **Greek**
  - Modern Greek
  - Albanian
- **Latin**
  - Romanian
  - Portuguese
  - Spanish
  - Catalan
  - Occitan
  - French
  - Italian
- **Germanic**
  - Dutch, Afrikaans, etc.
  - Plattdeutsch
  - English, American
  - Frisian
  - Yiddish
  - German
  - Norwegian, etc.
  - Swedish, Danish
  - Armenian
- **Iranian**
  - Kurdish, Farsi, etc.
  - Avestan
- **Indian**
  - Bengali, etc.
  - Hindi

THE STORY OF WRITING

The earliest writing system is called cuneiform. It was invented and used by the peoples of Mesopotamia about 4,500 years ago. They used a wedge to make marks on a piece of wet clay. A similar system, called hieroglyphics, was used in Ancient Egypt. The Egyptians carved pictures and symbols on monuments and tombs, telling of great deeds or offering prayers to their gods. They also used hieratic writing. This consisted of painting colored pictures and symbols on to papyrus.

Much later, in Central America, the Maya people invented their own hieroglyphic writing system.

The first true alphabet, based on cuneiform and hieroglyphic writing, was used by the Ancient Greeks. The Greek alphabet, created about 1,000 BC, spread to many parts of the world. It was the direct ancestor of the Latin and Cyrillic alphabets. Modern English uses the Latin alphabet.

The Arabic alphabet has 28 letters and is written from right to left.

Chinese writing is quite different to our Latin alphabet. It uses a large number of characters, each of which has its own separate meaning.

Cuneiform writing from Ancient Mesopotamia.

Maya hieroglyphic writing.

Ancient Egyptian hieroglyphic writing.

Latin writing from a medieval manuscript.

Sixteenth-century Arabic. This is the tugra (signature) of the Turkish sultan Süleyman the Magnificent.

Chinese character, meaning 'eternity'.

A man of Chinese origin reading a bilingual English-Spanish newspaper in New York.

World languages

When people who speak different languages want to talk they can either use interpreters or speak a second language they both know.

At present, English is the most common international language. Business people, scientists, students, and tourists all use English to communicate with others who don't speak their language.

In the past, attempts have been made to invent special world languages, such as Esperanto, but these have never been very successful.

Braille

In 1824 a blind man called Louis Braille invented a system of writing for blind people. Braille consists of 63 characters, each made up of raised dots. Blind people "read" these characters by passing their fingers lightly over the paper with the dots.

Children learn to use computers at school. They are often more skilled at using them than their parents.

Language and technology

Technological progress over the last 200 years has dramatically increased the speed with which people can communicate. Early forms of long-distance communication included drumming in Africa, or smoke signals among Native Americans. Inventions like the telegraph and telephone in the 19th century, and the radio, television, fax, and the internet last century have changed the way people live and work. The internet is perhaps one of the most revolutionary inventions yet. On the net, people from around the world can exchange information using their computers.

Signals and symbols

For quick communication and convenience, people sometimes agree that a certain word, or shape, or color, has a special meaning. Road signs and traffic lights are a good example of this. Throughout most of the world green means "go", and red "stop".

Conflict in the Middle East

The Middle East has always been inhabited by a variety of different ethnic and religious groups. Tolerance has often been a keynote in allowing contrasting cultures to exist side by side. Even so, in recent years the attempt to squeeze opposing groups into the boundaries of modern states has often led to conflict. In Lebanon, for example, civil war between Muslim and Christian groups has all but destroyed the country's economy.

Lebanese children play on an abandoned tank.

The suq is a favorite meeting place for men, who gather in tiny cafés to chat.

The suq
Muslims cities are centered around the mosque and the suq, or marketplace.

Palestine
Modern Israel was founded in Palestine where Arab Palestinians had been living for centuries. They bitterly opposed the formation of a Jewish State, and many were forced to flee to refugee camps when Israel was formed in 1948. Some Palestinians have lived their whole lives in these camps. Recent developments may lead to the formation of a separate Palestinian state on the West Bank and the Gaza Strip.

Iran
Since 1979, Iran (previously Persia) has been governed by Muslim religious leaders according to the strict laws of the Koran.

Iraq
Known for many centuries as Mesopotamia, the history of Iraq stretches back to the origins of human civilization. Modern Iraqis are mainly Arabs. Most of them are Shiite Muslims.

Decoration from the ancient city of Persepolis, founded about 500 BC.

Image from the Hammurabi stela, named after a Babylonian ruler who recorded one of the earliest codes of law, nearly 4,000 years ago.

Solar-powered telephone in a desert in Kuwait.

The "Promised Land"
When Jerusalem fell to Roman rule in 70 BC, most Jews left their homeland in Palestine to live in Europe, Asia, or Africa. When the modern state of Israel was formed in 1948, it seemed to many to be the answer to a prayer that they and their ancestors had recited for more than 2,000 years.

Orthodox Jew reads from the Torah.

Black gold
Many countries in the Middle East have rich deposits of petroleum. The largest sources are in Saudia Arabia, Kuwait, Qatar, and the United Arab Emirates. Exporting oil has become an important business for these countries and many have been able to develop their economies with oil-earned revenues.

Tradition and change
Despite Western influence, many Arab countries maintain and enforce strict Islamic laws. In some countries, for example, women are not only forced to wear veils, but they are also not allowed to drive cars.

Mecca
For Muslims, Mecca is the holiest of all cities. The Prophet Muhammad, the founder of Islam, was born here in 570. It is an important religious center and all Muslims try to make at least one *hajj*, or pilgrimage, here during their lifetimes.

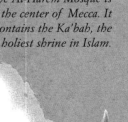

The Al-Harem Mosque is in the center of Mecca. It contains the Ka'bah, the holiest shrine in Islam.

Qatan man from Saudi Arabia.

Saudi Arabia
Wealth and jobs generated by oil have attracted migrant workers from other countries of the Middle East and also from Muslim countries in Southeast Asia and Africa.

Fishermen
The inhabitants of Yemen and Oman, countries facing the Indian Ocean, have always been fishermen as well as farmers. Recently their governments have tried to encourage this activity in an attempt to increase exports.

Kurdish girl in traditional costume.

The Kurds – a stateless people

The Kurds have lived in the Taurus and Zagrus Mountains for centuries, in an area that is known as Kurdistan ("Land of the Kurds"). But when modern states were formed, no special area was set aside for the them. Nowadays an estimated 17 million Kurds live divided between Turkey, Iran, Iraq, Syria, and Armenia. They have been harshly treated by these countries on many occasions.

SYRIA
Pop. 15,200,000
Cap. Damascus

LEBANON
Pop. 3,100,000
Cap. Beirut

ISRAEL
Pop. 5,800,000
Cap. Jerusalem

JORDAN
Pop. 5,700,000
Cap. Amman

IRAN
Pop. 68,700,000
Cap. Tehran

AFGHANISTAN
Pop. 21,500,000
Cap. Kabul

IRAQ
Pop. 21,000,000
Cap. Baghdad

KUWAIT
Pop. 1,600,000
Cap. Kuwait City

UNITED ARAB EMIRATES
Pop. 1,900,000
Cap. Abu Dhabi

OMAN
Pop. 2,300,000
Cap. Muscat

QATAR
Pop. 400,000
Cap. Doha

SAUDI ARABIA
Pop. 19,400,000
Cap. Riyadh

YEMEN
Pop. 15,100,000
Cap. Sana

BAHRAIN
Pop. 505,000
Cap. Manama

Afghanistan

The peoples of Afghanistan are a mosaic of cultures and languages. The Pashtun form the largest ethnic group. The official languages are Pashto and Dari. Most Afghans live as farmers. About one-fifth lead nomadic lives. With the withdrawal of Soviet troops in 1989, the country has been plunged into civil war.

Oriental carpets

Carpets are woven all over the Middle East. They are used as prayer mats, for receiving guests, and for sleeping on. Many localities pride themselves on a special design or quality of carpet. They are also an important export item.

Desert lands

Much of the Middle East is covered with arid lands or desert. For centuries the camel has been an important means of transport and a respected source of food and wealth.

Veiled Bedouin woman.

Bedouin

The Bedouin are an Arab-speaking people of the deserts of the Middle East. Originally nomads, recent governments have forced many of them to settle in one place.

Girl from Dhofar in Oman.

Oman

The people of Oman are mainly Arab, but there are also many Indian, African, Iranian, and Western workers in the country. Most people live in rural areas.

Yemen

The fortress houses of Yemen, built of stone, mud, and brick, and sometimes as high as six stories, are symbolic of a people who have often had to face invasion and civil war.

The Middle East

The Middle East consists of the countries of the Arabian Peninsula, Iran, and Afghanistan. This area is sometimes called the cradle of human civilization because it was here that people first became farmers, growing crops and keeping domestic animals. The world's earliest civilizations grew up in the fertile valley between the Tigris and Euphrates rivers. The Sumerians appeared about 3500 BC. They developed the earliest writing system and founded an empire based around a group of cities. They were followed by the Assyrians, the Babylonians, and the Persians. Over the centuries their cities became vital centers on trade routes which linked Europe, Asia, and India. Three world religions – Judaism, Christianity, and Islam – all began in this area. The Muslims conquered the region in the 7th century and almost all its inhabitants were converted to Islam. The majority of people are still Muslim today. The area remained under Arab and Ottoman control until early in the 20th century, when the modern states gradually emerged. The Middle East was torn by conflict during much of the 20th century. The founding of the Jewish State of Israel in 1948 was bitterly opposed by many Arab countries. The increasing importance of oil in the world economy has made some countries extremely rich in the last few decades. Arabic is the most widely spoken language, among many others.

Central Asia and Siberia

Central Asia and Siberia occupy a vast area, from the Ural Mountains in the west to the Pacific Ocean in the east, and from China and Mongolia in the south to the Arctic Ocean in the north. The natural environment is hostile, with deserts, steppes, taiga (subarctic forest), and tundra, and harsh climatic conditions. The first humans settled here about 30,000 years ago. The early peoples of Siberia lived in isolated clan groups. They were nomadic herders of sheep, horses, and reindeer, or hunters and gatherers. Agriculture was unknown until the arrival of Russian settlers.

In Central Asia there were both sedentary farmers and nomadic herders. Cities emerged where the herders and farmers could exchange goods. Some cities, such as Bukhara and Samarkand, became important market towns on the great trade routes that linked Europe with India and China. They were immensely wealthy and became important centers of learning, where history, astronomy, mathematics, medicine, and poetry were studied and taught. During the 16th to 19th centuries, Russia gradually conquered both Siberia and Central Asia. Russian influence and settlers gradually spread south and east. The Soviet Union encompassed both regions after the Revolution in 1917, changing them dramatically by bringing heavy industry and a military presence. After the collapse of the Soviet Union in the early 1990s, the countries of Central Asia achieved independence. Siberia remains a part of Russia and ethnic Russians are the largest group in Siberia today.

KAZAKHSTAN
Pop. 17,200,000
Cap. Astana

UZBEKISTAN
Pop. 23,300,000
Cap. Tashkent

TURKMENISTAN
Pop. 4,200,000
Cap. Ashkhabad

KIRGHIZIA
Pop. 4,800,000
Cap. Bishkek

TAJIKISTAN
Pop. 6,300,000
Cap. Dushanbe

SIBERIA (RUSSIA)
Pop. 148,000,000
Cap. Moscow

Nganasan hunter preparing frozen fish.

The peoples of Central Asia
The Turkic-speaking peoples of Central Asia have lived here for at least 2,000 years. They came to the area from Mongolia.

Tajikistan
Most people in Tajikistan live in country villages called *qishlaqs.* Like the other new Central Asian republics, the population is growing rapidly; over half the inhabitants are under twenty.

Tossing raw cotton in Tajikistan.

Cotton in Central Asia
Cotton is the most important export item in Central Asia. Huge canals have been dug to carry water to the cotton fields. Much of the hard work is still done by hand.

Folding yurts
Traditional herding peoples in Kazakhstan live in yurts, which can be folded away or put up in just a few hours. They are erected in grassy valleys where stock can graze. When the grass is eaten up, they move on to another spot.

Uzbekistan
For its mix of peoples and cultures, Uzbekistan is typical of the region. There are about 60 different ethnic groups in the country. Uzbeks make up around two-thirds of the population. Russians are a large minority group.

Uzbek man.

Turkmenistan
Turkmen were nomadic pastoralists, living in tent villages and raising goats, sheep, horses, camels, and cattle. The Soviet Government encouraged them to settle. Many now work in industry.

Protective clothing is worn when mining mineral salts. Turkmenistan is one of the world's largest sources of sodium sulfate, which is used to make glass, paper, and detergents.

Life in the Siberian north
Ways of life have changed greatly for the peoples of the North. But strong family ties and an increasing sense of their right to live in traditional ways help people face the future positively.

Kirghizia
Traditionally nomadic, the Kirghiz were forced to settle during Soviet rule. Even so, many age-old traditions survive. The recital of the *Manas*, an epic poem of more than 300,000 verses, is one of these.

Reciting the Manas *epic. The bards recite from memory for more than four hours.*

Mosque in Samarkand. Islam is the most widespread religion in Central Asia.

Samarkand
The ancient city of Samarkand was the most important economic and cultural center in Central Asia during the 14th to 16th centuries.

Pollution

Large-scale industrial development in Siberia has profoundly affected the natural environment. Industrial waste has devastated rivers and forests. In the early 1990s the government admitted that 16 percent of the area was so badly polluted that it was dangerous for people to live there.

Drilling for oil in the freezing Siberian winter.

Siberia's wealth

Siberia covers 5 million square miles and has just over 25 million inhabitants. It has very rich deposits of natural gas, oil, and other minerals. Many people from European Russia brave the harsh climate and isolation because they can find work in the mines and factories.

Yupik peoples

Yupiks live in eastern Siberia. They are related to the Aleut and Inuit people of North America.

Yupik hunter in the Bering Strait.

Bear festival in the Ural Mountains.

Kamchatka

The Kamchatka peninsula is now inhabited mainly by Russians who live by catching crabs, and canning them for export. Indigenous peoples include the Koryak and Itelmen.

The Yakut

The Yakuts are a large ethnic group in Siberia. They speak a Turkic language, and linguists think that they migrated here from the south. They have almost completely adopted Russian ways of life. They live by keeping cattle, fishing, and hunting.

Yakut hunting mask, for protection in the snow.

Hunting rites

Hunting rites were important in traditional Siberian societies. Before bear hunting expeditions, for example, the hunters held a special ceremony to ensure that the animal would not harm them. Today, local festivals recall ancient traditions.

Buryats - northern Mongols

The Buryats are related to the peoples of Mongolia. They live near Lake Baikal, in southern Siberia. Their traditional religion is a mixture of Buddhism and Shamanism.

Buryat woman dressed in traditional costume for a festival.

Koryak woman from the Kamchatka peninsula.

Hawker in Kirghizia.

Religion in Siberia

All religious practices were discouraged under Soviet rule. Even so, traditional Shamanist, Buddhist, Christian, and Muslim beliefs continued. Since the early 1990s there has been an upsurge in religious worship.

Buddhist monk.

Eveny reindeer herder in northeast Siberia.

Hawking

Hawking, or hunting with a hawk, falcon, or eagle, is an ancient sport in Central Asia and southern Siberia. Local epics and popular traditions include many references to the sport.

Baby sleds

Going to school in sub zero temperatures calls for some special technology. In the Arctic regions, some parents use covered sleds to take their children out.

The end of a way of life?

Reindeer herding was a way of life for many indigenous peoples of northern Siberia. Family groups lived wandering lives as they followed the reindeer herds that provided them with food, clothing, and shelter. After the 1930s the Soviet Government took over many herds and forced the people to live in villages. In some areas only the men herd now. They are away from their families for long periods and their children are not learning herding skills. Forestry and farming have drastically reduced the area over which the reindeer range. Reindeer herding may gradually die out.

China and Mongolia

Just over one-fifth of the population of the world lives in China, an area only slightly larger than the United States. The story of China is very old. It has been inhabited continuously for over 500,000 years. Traces of the earliest modern people have been dated to about 30,000 years ago. The first farms developed in the Hwang Ho (Yellow River) and the Yangtze (Blue River) valleys in 7000 BC, while the first written records date from about 4,000 years ago. China was united under the Ch'in dynasty in 221 BC, and by then it had efficient political and administrative systems and many towns. Chinese civilization, based primarily on agriculture, remained isolated from the rest of the world until the collapse of the last dynasty in 1911. After a period of unrest, the Communist Party took control in 1949 and remains in power to the present day. The official language is Mandarin, and while religion is frowned upon by the communist regime, traditional Buddhist and Confucian beliefs continue. Mongolia lies to the north of China. It is very thinly populated, mainly by Khalkha-speaking Mongols. Turkic languages, Russian, and Chinese are also spoken. Buddhism is the predominant religion. Traditionally Mongolians were rural pastoralists (often nomadic), but nowadays almost half the population lives in towns. The annual Naadam festival of the Three Games of Men (wrestling, archery, and horse racing) is the most famous celebration of traditional ways.

MONGOLIA
Pop. 2,500,000
Cap. Ulan Bator
CHINA
Pop. 1,240,000,000
Cap. Beijing
MACAU
(Portugal)
Pop. 480,000

Mongol woman in traditional costume, with a bowl of milk as a religious offering.

Religion in Mongolia
Mongolia was fervently Buddhist until the Republic of Mongolia was formed in 1924. Before then over half the men had been monks and there were more than 700 monasteries.

Tibet
Tibet was an independent country until the Chinese invaded in 1950. Isolated from the rest of the world, its people spoke the Tibetan language and practiced Tibetan Buddhism. The Dalai Lama, spiritual leader of the country, was forced into exile in 1959. The Tibetans have strongly resisted Chinese pressure to abandon their culture, and during the 1980s China eased up a little in its attempts to change their ways.

Tibetan prayermill
Prayer is extremely important for Tibetan Buddhists. Many use prayermills, small rotating cylinders with prayers on them, which they swing clockwise to pray.

Tsam religious ceremonies
The tsam dance is typical of Mongolia. Of Tibetan origin, the masked dancers are believed to frighten away evil spirits and appease the gods.

Chinese agriculture
Agriculture forms the basis of the Chinese economy. About two-thirds of the population work on farms. Rice is the most important crop and a staple food in the Chinese diet.

Tibetan Buddhist monk. His yellow hat shows that he follows reformed beliefs.

The martial arts
Kung fu, judo, and karate all originated in China. They are closely linked to Zen Buddhism and Taoism.

Terrace farming is common on steep hillsides, where it prevents erosion.

Tibetan Buddhism
Buddhism in Tibet differs from Buddhism in other Asian countries because it contains many traces of earlier Tibetan beliefs.

This man is a Buddhist pilgrim on a visit to Sera Monastery near Lhasa. Sticking out one's tongue is a traditional salute, showing respect.

The Mongol people

The Mongols, descendants of the military leader Genghis Khan, who conquered China in the 13th century, lived as nomads until a few decades ago. Recent industrial growth has brought many people to the cities to work.

For traditional Mongolians the horse is central to their way of life, providing both transport and food.

The Great Wall

The red line shows the Great Wall of China. About 4,000 miles long, it was probably built as a defense system to keep northern nomadic tribes out of China.

A tower on the Great Wall.

Actors in costume perform traditional Beijing opera.

Chinese theater

Theater is the most important popular art in China. Contemporary Cantonese and Beijing operas feature elaborate costumes, song, dance, martial arts, and acrobatics.

Ethnic minorities

There are 55 official minority groups in China, including the Muslim Hui of the northeast, the Chuang in the southeast, and the Miao-Yao in the southwest. The Chinese government has encouraged self-government and autonomy for many of these groups.

Kazakh boy in traditional costume, in the Sinkiang region.

Limiting population growth

The Chinese government has been trying to limit the steadily increasing population since the 1950s. The latest program, which began in 1979, seeks to encourage each family to have just one child. Efforts have been effective and China now has an unusually low population growth rate for a developing country.

Chinese literature

China has one of the oldest literary traditions in the world, beginning from about 3,000 years ago. An early classic, called the *Shih Ching* ("Classic of Poetry"), is an anthology dating from the time of Confucius, about 500 BC.

Two verses by the poet Wang Wei (699-759).

The Hall of Supreme Harmony in the Forbidden City, Beijing.

The Forbidden City

The 9,000 rooms of the Imperial Palace complex in Beijing housed the Chinese Emperor and his court until 1911. It was called the Forbidden City because no foreigner or commoner was allowed to enter. After the communists came to power in 1949, the palaces were made into museums and opened to the public.

The sampan

Sampans are used on the many canals, rivers, and lakes of China by merchants and traders. They can be propelled by a single bamboo oar or, more recently, by a small outboard motor.

Hong Kong

After 99 years as a British Crown Colony, Hong Kong was returned to China in 1997. It has one of the busiest ports in the world, and is a bustling center of trade, finance, manufacturing, and tourism.

The Han majority

About 94 percent of the Chinese people share the same traditions, culture, and written language. This group is called the Han. Mandarin is the most common spoken language.

Tradition and change

China remains a Communist country with a centrally planned economy and strong official dislike of the capitalist West. Even so, in recent years China has slowly begun to change. Particularly in some of the larger cities, a more Western-style economy is slowly making itself felt.

Religions

The evidence, from the earliest records of the first people to the present day, shows that humans have always felt a need to believe in supernatural powers that govern nature and control their destiny. Regardless of whether the supernatural power may be perceived as a group of spirits or gods, or a single god, people have prayed and offered gifts to them. They have also built shrines, altars, temples, and statues in their honor. These beliefs, and the practices and traditions bound up with them, constitute religion. As far as we know, there has never been a human society that did not have some kind of religion. There are, however, individuals who don't believe in supernatural powers. They are called atheists.

Sacred texts
Nearly all religions have sacred texts. They are usually collections telling the life and teachings of the founder of the religion, or the exploits of its gods. The oldest surviving sacred texts are the Vedas, written in India over 3,000 years ago.

Ancient religions
Most ancient religions were polytheistic, which means that more than one god was worshiped. In monotheistic religions only one god is worshiped.

RELIGIONS OF THE WORLD

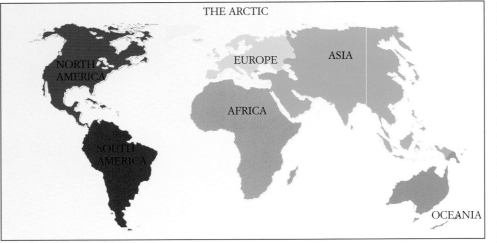

THE ARCTIC

NORTH AMERICA

EUROPE

ASIA

AFRICA

SOUTH AMERICA

OCEANIA

Arctic
About 1 million indigenous people live in the Arctic Circle. Primal religions thrive along with Christian faiths brought by settlers and missionaries from the 17th century onward.

North America
Christian faiths predominate in North America. 97 percent of Latin Americans, 47 percent of Canadians and 21 percent of US citizens are Roman Catholic. The majority of Americans claim Protestantism as their faith: Baptist, Episcopal, Lutheran, Methodist, Presbyterianism and others. Jewish communities exist in all metropolitan centers, as well as smaller pockets of Muslims, Hindus, and Buddhists.

Europe
Catholicism and Protestantism are the main faiths in Western Europe. There are significant Islamic populations in France, Hindus in the United Kingdom, and Jewish communities in many metropolitan centers. The major Eastern European religions include Eastern Orthodoxy, Roman Catholicism, and Islam.

Australasia and the Pacific Islands
Protestant faiths are in the majority in Australia and New Zealand. There is also a large Catholic population and primal religions are practiced by traditional peoples throughout the region.

South America
About 90 percent of South Americans are Roman Catholic. Hindus and Muslims are present in the Asian immigrant communities in Suriname and Guyana.

Africa
Islam in the main religion in the north and north-east of Africa. Primal religions predominate below the Sahara, although Islam and Christian faiths are also practiced.

Asia
The major religions of the world began in Asia – Judaism, Christianity, and Islam in the Middle East; Buddhism, Hinduism, and Sikhism in India; Taoism and Confucianism in China; and Shinto in Japan.

Worship
All religions include forms of worship. Some common types of worship are prayer, meditation, dancing, sacred music and song, sermons, and veneration of people and objects. Acts of worship seek to unite the believer with the supernatural power or god.

Prayer is one of the most basic and universal forms of worship. Muslims kneel and, facing in the direction of Mecca, pray five times every day.

In Mexico on the Day of the Dead, (November 2nd), people make sweet edible skulls for the children to eat.

At the age of 13, Jewish boys recite passages from the Torah, thus signifying their religious coming-of-age. This ceremony, called the Bar Mitzva, is an important moment in the boys' lives.

Religious ceremonies and festivals
Important moments in human life, such as birth, reaching maturity, marriage, and death, are usually celebrated in religious ceremonies. Religious festivals are often held to remember or commemorate an important event in the life of a prophet or founder of a religion. For example, Christians celebrate Jesus' birthday at Christmas and his death and resurrection at Easter. Religious ceremonies and festivals are usually enjoyable occasions, where people stay together in groups with music, dance, and song.

The Taoist yin-yang symbol.

Taoism
Taoism originated in China over 2,500 years ago. Taoist beliefs emphasize freedom of the individual and respect for nature. Taoist thought divides the world into the feminine *yin*, which is cold and passive, and the masculine *yang*, which is hot and active.

Confucianism
Confucianism is a way of looking at the world and a way of life. It falls somewhere between a religion and a philosophy. It originated in China about 2,500 years ago when a man called Confucius (551-479 BC) gathered Chinese thought and tradition for later generations.

Confucius.

The Star of David has become a symbol for Judaism.

Judaism
Judaism is the oldest monotheistic religion in the world. According to Jewish tradition, it began when God made a pact with Abraham, promising his people a homeland and eternal salvation in exchange for exclusive loyalty to him. The story of the Jews is recorded in the Old Testament of the Bible. Traditional Jewish law derives from the first five books of the Bible, known as the Torah. The Talmud, a book of commentary and interpretations is also important.

Martin Luther led a breakaway from the Catholic Church. This caused the Reformation and the rise of the Protestant Church.

Christianity
Christianity is the most widespread religion and has the largest number of followers. It is founded on the teachings of Christ, who was born in Palestine about 2,000 years ago. He is believed to be the son of God, sent to Earth to save humanity. Christian doctrine is collected in the Old and New Testaments of the Bible. Over the centuries Christianity has split into many different movements. The main ones are Catholicism, Eastern Orthodoxy, and Protestantism.

Eastern Orthodoxy thrives in Russia, Eastern Europe, and the Balkans. The Orthodox churches in each country are independent, but they all maintain the Orthodox tradition.

The Pope is the head of the Roman Catholic Church based in the Vatican City in Rome, Italy.

Buddhism
Buddhism was founded in India by Gautama Siddhartha, a warrior prince who lived from 560-480 BC. Gautama became the Buddha, which means "Enlightened One", after years of meditation. Over the centuries Buddhism spread throughout Asia. It was adapted and changed according to the conditions in each country and now has many different forms.

Statue of Buddha.

There are two main groups within Islam: the Sunnite majority and the Shiite movement. Smaller offshoots include the Dervishes, a mystical brotherhood who fall into whirling dancing trances in order to come into contact with their god.

Muhammad.

Islam
Islam is based on the preachings of Muhammad, who lived in Arabia between 570-632 AD. He claimed that Allah gave him the Koran, Islam's sacred text, and the task of converting non-believers. Islam is now one of the most widespread religions in the world. Every Muslim has five duties, called the pillars of Islam: the declaration of faith, prayer five times a day, giving to the poor, fasting during the month of Ramadan, and a pilgrimage to Mecca, the birthplace of Muhammad.

Primal religions
Many traditional peoples believe in a world of spirits and beings stronger than themselves. Some of these beings are considered friendly and can be asked for help to win a battle or to increase the yield of a farmer's field. Others are seen as evil and responsible for disease and misfortune. These can be offered sacrifices and prayer. Most traditional peoples also believe that the spirits of those who have died live on, and they practice ancestor worship. The variety of primal religions is as great as the number of traditional peoples since each has its own special set of beliefs.

Hopi Indian statue of a spiritual guardian.

Brahmin reading sacred Hindu text.

Shinto
Shinto is the native religion of Japan. It consists of a variety of religious practices and is closely linked to the story of Japan. Sacred texts, such as the *Kojiki*, tell how Japan was founded by the gods Izanagi and Izanami. It is not an exclusive religion and many Japanese are followers of both Shinto and other religions.

Hinduism
The Hindu religion is intertwined with the history and traditions of India where it is still practiced today. It is a very old religion, dating back about 4,000 years. It has no founder, no prophets, and no institutional order. The gods people worship, the festivals they celebrate, and their beliefs, vary greatly. Even so, some ideas are shared by all Hindus. One of these is reincarnation, or rebirth. Hindus believe that when people die they are born again, either as a person or as some other form of life. The process of death and rebirth continues until they free themselves. Shiva, Krishna, and Vishnu are three of the most well-known gods.

Female Shinto priest at a shrine.

The Indian Subcontinent

BANGLADESH
Pop. 123, 000,000
Cap. Dacca

BHUTAN
Pop. 1,700,000
Cap. Thimphu

NEPAL
Pop. 22,500,000
Cap. Katmandu

PAKISTAN
Pop. 136,800,000
Cap. Islamabad

INDIA
Pop. 975,800,000
Cap. New Delhi

MALDIVES
Pop. 254,000
Cap. Malé

SRI LANKA
Pop. 18,600,000
Cap. Colombo

The Indian Subcontinent is home to more than 1.2 billion people, or one-fifth of the population of the world. It is bounded in the north by the Himalayas, the tallest mountains in the world, and in the south by the Indian Ocean. Its peoples speak more than 600 different languages.

It has been invaded many times over the centuries. The earliest Aryan invaders were followed by Mogul Muslims and Europeans. The original Dravidian peoples were driven into southern India, where their descendants still live today. Successive waves of immigration have created a rich and varied culture. Intensely religious, in 5,000 years they have given life to four major religions – Hinduism, Jainism, Buddhism, and Sikhism, and adopted several others, including Islam and Christianity.

India was a British colony for almost a century until it gained independence in 1947. Because of religious differences, it split into predominantly Hindu India and majority Muslim East and West Pakistan. East Pakistan became independent Bangladesh in 1971.

The largest democracy in Asia, India is a startling mixture of tradition and progress. Sri Lanka in the south, and Bhutan and Nepal in the north, are predominantly Buddhist countries.

Pakistan, an Islamic state
Ninety-seven percent of the population of Pakistan are Muslims. Strict Islamic codes are more often observed in rural areas. This woman is wearing a traditional veil, so that only her hands are visible.

Veiled Muslim woman.

Sikhism, a young religion
Sikhism was founded in the 15th century. It borrowed from Hinduism and Islam to form a unique new religion. Most Sikhs live in the Punjab.

Oxen used for farm work.

Sacred cows
Most Indians live in country villages and live as farmers. They use oxen and water-buffalo for heavy farm work but do not eat beef. Hindus consider the cow a sacred animal and cows often wander freely through villages and countryside.

Hindu woman in traditional sari dress.

Nomadic Khanabadosh snake-charmer.

The Ganges, a holy river
Many rivers are holy for Hindus, but "Mother Ganga" in northern India, is the holiest of them all. Every year millions of pilgrims make long journeys to wash away their sins in its sacred waters. Varanasi (Benares), is the holiest city on the Ganges and the most popular pilgrim town.

Nomads
About 7 percent of Indians are nomads. Of many different languages, religions and races, they wander the backroads of India, earning their livings by keeping sheep or goats, as tinkers, or by entertaining the local inhabitants as magicians and snake-charmers.

Ladakhis
In the cold, upland valleys of the Himalayas, the Ladakhi peoples dress in warm woolen robes. The women often wear a richly decorated hat, called a *perak*.

Ladakhi girl.

Naga peoples
The Naga peoples live in Nagaland in northeast India. They speak many different dialects and live mainly as farmers.

Punjab man in distinctive white turban.

The Punjab
The Punjab was divided between Pakistan and India in 1947. The people speak either Punjabi or Hindi.

Sherpas
The Sherpa people live in the Himalayas. Of Tibetan descent, they cross the mountains into Tibet carrying rice which they trade for salt.

Naga boy.

Rajastan
Villagers in rural Rajastan still wear traditional white *dhotis* and colorful turbans to keep them cool in this desert region.

Buddha's awakening
Siddharta Gautama, founder of the Buddhist religion, was awakened and became the Buddha at Bodh Gaya.

Mahabodhi Temple.

The Taj Mahal
The Mogul Emperor, Shah Jahan built this tomb for his beloved wife in the 17th century. It is one of the finest examples of Mogul architecture.

The Vina
The *vina* is a stringed musical instrument, similar to the better-known sitar.

Shiva
One of the three great Hindu gods, Shiva is seen as both the destroyer and re-creator of human life. He is often shown with many hands.

Shiva dancing in a ring of fire.

Parsis
The Parsis, followers of the Zoroastrian religion, left Persia in the 8th century to escape religious persecution by Muslims. A small community in India, they live mainly in Bombay.

Parsi boy in traditional dress.

Tamil woman
The southern Tamils are the descendants of the original Dravidian peoples. They are fiercely proud of their language and culture.

The southern temples
The state of Tamil Nadu in the south has hundreds of traditional Hindu temples.

Mylapur Temple.

The Maldives
Maldivians are descendants of peoples from India and Sri Lanka. The official language is Divehi, but they also speak Arabic, Hindi, and English. Only a minority of the coral islands are inhabited.

Sri Lanka
The Sinhalese are the main ethnic group in Sri Lanka. Sinhala, Tamil, and English are widely spoken.

Sinhalese aristocrat at a Buddhist festival in Sri Lanka.

Ganesh
The elephant-headed god, Ganesh, is the son of Shiva. His elephant head symbolizes intelligence and strength.

Ganesh.

Japan, Korea and Taiwan

JAPAN
Pop. 126,300,000
Cap. Tokyo

TAIWAN
Pop. 21,600,000
Cap. Taipei

NORTH KOREA
Pop. 24,300,000
Cap. Pyongyang

SOUTH KOREA
Pop. 45,400,000
Cap. Seoul

The islands of Japan and the Korean peninsula were populated by people from Asia about 30,000 years ago. The early inhabitants of Japan were among the first people in the world to make pottery. Beautiful pots and bowls have been dated to the Jomon period, about 10,000 years ago. Japan and Korea were influenced by Chinese culture. They used Chinese characters for writing, practiced Buddhism and Confucianism, and adopted Chinese forms of government. Over the centuries, both countries adapted what they had borrowed from China to create their own unique cultures. Because they remained isolated, resisting outside influence until the end of the 19th century, Japan and Korea still have strong and distinct national cultures.

The original inhabitants of Taiwan were from Malaysia and Polynesia. These indigenous peoples now make up only about 2 percent of the population. The vast majority are of Chinese origin and Mandarin is the official language. Korea is divided into North Korea and South Korea. The North is a communist country, the South is democratic. Since the 1950s, Japan, South Korea, and Taiwan have all experienced huge economic growth. Improved economic conditions and increasing trade with the West are changing the traditional way of life.

The Ainu – An endangered people

A few thousand Ainu people survive on the northern island of Hokkaido. The Ainu don't belong to the same ethnic group as the Japanese. They used to live on all four islands, but have been gradually pushed north. Over the centuries they have intermarried with Japanese people, and their language and culture are now almost entirely lost.

Ainu woman, with traditional blue tattooing around her mouth.

Samurai sword, or daito.

Samurai

The Samurai were a group of warriors who rose to power and dominated Japanese government for hundreds of years. Samurai culture gave rise to some uniquely Japanese arts, such as the tea ceremony and flower arranging.

Food and religion in Japan

Japanese food has been strongly influenced by Buddhist and Shinto beliefs. Red meat, for example, is often considered a vulgar food, less desirable than fish, shellfish, or seaweed. The simple way in which dishes are presented and the tendency to maintain ingredients as close as possible to their natural state are based on Shintoist ideas of sincerity and respect for nature.

Traditional clothing

Many men and women still wear beautiful kimonos, particularly on special or ceremonial occasions. After a ritual bath, the wearer first puts on a dazzling white robe. The colorful kimono goes over the top. It is secured by a sash at the waist, called an *obi*.

Sumo

Sumo is a traditional form of Japanese wrestling. It is an old sport, but still very popular today. The wrestlers, wearing only loincloths, face each other on a small wooden platform. The winner, following traditional moves, has to push his opponent out of bounds. Sumo wrestlers are huge, some weighing 400 pounds or more.

Confucianism in Korea

Confucian thought has strongly influenced Korean society. Even today, the South Korean government periodically exhorts its citizens not to commit crimes, and to avoid showy displays of wealth and privilege.

Traditional male clothing in Korea.

North Korea

Since it came to power in 1948, the Communist Government has outlawed religion and repressed many other aspects of traditional culture. North Korea remains isolated from the rest of the world.

Korean cuisine

As in the rest of Asia, rice is the staple dish. The second most popular dish is *Kimch'i*, a spicy mixture of garlic, peppers, and vegetables or seafood.

The Korean alphabet

Koreans originally came from central and northern Asia. The unique language they brought with them is thought to be distantly related to Turkic and Mongolian tongues. In 1446 Koreans decided that the Chinese script could not adequately express their language, so they invented a new alphabet. A great celebration was held on October 9, 1446, the day it was introduced. A national holiday is still held every year on that date.

Japan and the West

For a long time Japan remained closed to Western influence. Foreigners were forbidden entry and the Christian religion was outlawed. These restrictions were abolished in 1868 and Japanese people began to meet Europeans and Americans. The impact was great and many Western habits and customs have been adopted.

A world economic power

Japanese industry was a world economic leader beginning at the end of the 19th century. Manufactured goods were exported around the world. World War II left the country in ruins and its industry had to start over. Japan rebuilt its economy and made its presence felt in international trade. Today, it is one of the three most industrialized countries and is especially strong in high-tech manufacturing.

Religion

In Japan, Shinto, various sects of Buddhism, Christianity, and several new religions exist peacefully together. None of the religions is dominant and a person may, for example, believe in several Shinto gods and at the same time belong to a Buddhist sect. Similar situations exist in Korea and Taiwan, where Buddhism, Confucianism, Taoism, Christianity, and Shamanism co-exist harmoniously.

The torii of the Itsukushima shrine at Miyajima is one of the most famous Shinto shrines.

Shinto

Shinto is the native religion of Japan. It is closely linked to the world of nature. Shintoists worship spirits, called *kami*, and their ancestors. The *torii*, a decorative gateway, is the symbol of Shinto. It is usually placed at the entrance to a shrine, which may be a building or a simple field. There are no images in Shinto shrines. The spirit is represented by a mirror, which stands for the sun, light, and perfect sincerity.

Theater in Japan

There are many kinds of traditional theater in Japan. Two of the most famous are called *Kabuki* and *Noh*. *Kabuki* comes from the Japanese words for song (*ka*), dance (*bu*), and skill (*ki*). It dates from the 17th century and is still very popular. *Noh* theater dates back to the 15th century. It is more stylized and classic.

Women in Japan

In the past women were expected to leave their jobs when they married. This is changing slowly, but it is still unusual for a woman to reach a high position at work. Laws enforcing equal employment opportunities were introduced in Japan during the 1980s.

The problems of growth

In recent decades Taiwan has changed from being an agricultural country to an industrialized one. This has made most people richer, but has also brought problems. One of the most serious, particularly in Taipei, is air pollution.

Buddhism

Buddhism was introduced to Korea, Japan, and Taiwan by the Chinese. It is now an important religion in east Asia.

Buddhist monk.

The family in Taiwan

The family is very important in Taiwanese society. Families work together to improve the lives of everyone in the group. A family in Taiwan can include several generations all living together.

The economic miracle

The economic boom in the countries of east Asia is largely the result of hard work. Factory workers in South Korea work an average of about 55 hours per week, compared with 35-40 in the West.

The high-tech industry is important in the economies of all four countries.

Taiwanese bride in Western dress.

Father and son in Taipei with masks as protection against air pollution.

MYANMAR
Pop. 47,500,000
Cap. Rangoon

VIETNAM
Pop. 76,200,000
Cap. Hanoi

LAOS
Pop. 5,000,000
Cap. Vientiane

CAMBODIA
Pop. 10,500,000
Cap. Phnom Penh

PHILIPPINES
Pop. 69,000,000
Cap. Manila

THAILAND
Pop. 60,210,000
Cap. Bangkok

MALAYSIA
Pop. 20,600,000
Cap. Kuala Lumpur

SINGAPORE
Pop. 2,900,000
Cap. Singapore

BRUNEI
Pop. 300,000
Cap. Bandar
Seri Begawan

INDONESIA
Pop. 200,000,000
Cap. Jakarta

Long-necked beauty
Among the Padaung people of Myanmar, it is the custom to gradually stretch women's necks to up to 15 inches in length. This is done by applying an increasing number of brass rings to girls' necks from the age of five. According to tradition, the rings act as protection against tiger attacks.

Vietnamese woman chooses fish from a basket. After rice, fish is the second most important food staple.

Myanmar (Burma)
Over 100 different languages are spoken in Myanmar. Burmese is now the official language. The vast majority of Burmans are Buddhists.

Akha woman from the hills of northern Thailand. The women wear their colorful headgear not only on special occasions but also when they work in the fields.

Buddhist temple at Dogon.

Vietnam
Most people in Vietnam are employed on the land as farmers. They all speak the Vietnamese language, but Chinese, French, English, and Khmer are also widely spoken.

Religion in Southeast Asia
The main religions are Buddhism, Hinduism, and Islam. Primal religions are common among indigenous peoples. Christianity and Confucianism are widespread as well.

Huge statue of a reclining Buddha.

Thailand
The name "Thailand" translates as "the land of the free." It is the only country in Southeast Asia that was never colonized by Europeans. The main languages are Thai and Chinese. English is also widely spoken. Buddhism is the main religion, but Muslims, Confucians, Christians, and Sikhs are also present.

Fishing
Fishing is common throughout Southeast Asia, both on inland waterways and at sea. It is usually small scale, subsistence fishing rather than export-oriented.

Singapore
Singapore is one of the largest ports in the world and a thriving commercial center. The people of Singapore are mainly Chinese, but many Indian and English people live there as well.

Skyscrapers in Singapore.

Sewing rice seed by hand. Farm work in Southeast Asia is mainly done by people, rather than by machines.

Nias
The island of Nias lies off the coast of Sumatra (Indonesia). The people are of Malay origin and speak dialects of Malay-Polynesian languages. Their distinctive villages are built around stone paved streets. During religious ceremonies, the people dress up in elaborate clothing and jewelry.

Nias woman during a religious ceremony.

Stylized Wayang puppet.

Rice
The people of Southeast Asia are dependent on rice as a staple food. Rice is grown in submerged areas, called paddy fields. It is cooked in an endless variety of ways and served at almost every meal.

Shadow theater in Java
Shadow puppet theater, or *Wayang* (from the Javanese word for shadow), came from India with the spread of the Hindu religion. Dramas of famous Hindu epics are acted out in long, midnight-to-dawn performances. *Wayang* plays are performed on special days, such as birthdays and anniversaries.

Southeast Asia

Southeast Asia includes the Indochinese peninsula on the Asian mainland, and the many thousands of islands comprising Indonesia and the Philippines. The peoples and cultures of this area vary greatly. Traces of the first modern humans here have been dated to over 40,000 years ago. Indian and Chinese civilizations both influenced the peoples of Southeast Asia from about 200 AD. The Buddhist and Hindu religions, common throughout the region, came from India. From the 13th century onward, the Islamic religion also spread throughout the area. It is still one of the main religions today. During the first half of the 16th century, European powers (France, Holland, Portugal, Spain, England) colonialized every country except Thailand. By the second half of the 20th century, all the colonies had achieved independence, sometimes at the cost of long and bloody wars. After the colonial era, many countries endured periods of conflict and political unrest. Even today, some military regimes and dictatorships survive. In recent years some countries have experienced economic booms and improved standards of living and tourism is becoming increasingly important.

The Philippines
The archipelago of the Philippines is composed of over 7,000 islands. Because the Philippines was a Spanish colony for 333 years, followed by 48 years of US rule, the country has strong ties with the West. Over 70 different languages are spoken in the islands, although only Filipino and English are official languages.

Roman Catholic Cardinal of Filipino origin.

Religion
Unlike the other countries of Southeast Asia, and reflecting the influence of more than 300 years of Spanish rule, the majority of Filipinos are Roman Catholics.

Junk used for trading among the islands.

Muslims in the Philippines
A small percentage of Filipinos are Muslims. They are called Moros. Over the centuries they have fought for independence from the Catholic Philippines.

Muslim soldier, from the Moro National Liberation Front.

Indonesia
Over 300 ethnic groups, 250 languages, and every major religion of the planet are represented on the islands of Indonesia. It is one of the most culturally diverse areas on the planet.

Decorated plate, from Borneo in Indonesia.

Indigenous peoples
In isolated areas many different groups of indigenous peoples still live according to traditional lifestyles. They live in small tribal groups and hunt and gather their food as required.

Floating market places
Much of life in Southeast Asia unfolds on or near the water. Millions of people live on boats or in houses built on stilts lining the waterways. Floating markets are common, where people sell or exchange goods between boats, or sell to the inhabitants of nearby houses.

Mangyan father and son, on Mindanao Island, in the southern Philippines.

A Toradja house with typical sloping roof.

The Toradja people
The Toradja people live on the island of Sulawesi (Indonesia). According to tradition, their ancestors came from the sea and their richly decorated houses have sloping roofs pointing in the direction from which they came.

Dance and theater in Southeast Asia
Few areas of the world have such a variety of dance and theatrical forms, and as many groups performing regularly. In most performances music, dance, drama, song, and narrative are combined in an explosion of color, movement, and sound.

Masked dancer in Bali.

Food and Costume

Eating and caring for our bodies are two basic human activities. Without food and drink we would die, and grooming and clothing are essential for good health and protection from the elements. However, food and costume mean much more than just feeding or covering the body. Clothing and body ornaments reveal much about a person's age, social position, wealth, occupation, religious beliefs, marital status, and more. The endless variety of foods, and the ways in which they are chosen, prepared, and eaten, are also closely related to peoples' ways of life and religious beliefs.

Body decoration
On the Mentawai Islands in Indonesia, some of the inhabitants have their teeth filed to a point. A person with filed teeth is considered particularly attractive.

Tattoos
Tattooing the body is common in many societies. Most tattoos are permanent and can often be part of a rite of passage or simply a fashion statement.

Jewelry
Jewelry is usually made of gold or precious stones. A great deal of jewelry has been found in ancient tombs and buried underground, so we know that people have been wearing it for thousands of years. Necklaces, rings, and bracelets are still popular throughout the world today. Making, and wearing, jewelry has become a form of art. Some traditional peoples wear very elaborate jewelry. Often the wearer makes her own pieces from what she can find.

This young woman from Mali has combined silver, copper, brass, coins, lumps of amber, and glass beadwork in her elaborate headdress.

Fashion
Clothes, accessories, and jewelry all change over time. In Western societies, fashion can change very quickly, from one season to the next. The fashion industry has become an important business. In traditional societies dress styles usually change more slowly, often after people come into contact with new peoples or materials.

Costume and social position
Clothing not only serves to cover or protect the body, it also tells us about the wearer's social position. In most societies, very elaborate, richly decorated dress and accessories mean that the wearer is of high status.

The rich beading and the design of her tattoos reveal that this Kenyah woman from Malaysia is of high status. Her pierced and elongated ear lobes are typical of the Kenyah people.

Dress and occupation
Some jobs require special clothing or uniforms. Police officers, soldiers, pilots, laboratory technicians, waiters, construction workers, and many others, all wear uniforms or protective clothing on the job.

Doctors in hospitals usually wear a clean white coat.

Shoes
Shoes not only protect the feet, but their color, form, and use are also culturally significant. In Japan, outdoor shoes are not worn in the house. Family members exchange their shoes for *zori* (sandals) at the entrance. Guests are provided with special sandals.

Costume and religion
Religious followers sometimes wear special clothing, jewelry, or masks. A priest's cassock, or a cross worn about the neck, are two good examples from the Christian religion. This Gozak girl from Tibet is wearing 108 plaits. The number is sacred to Buddhists because there are 108 volumes of Buddha's writings.

A Yanomami woman prepares nutritious cassava flour from the manioc plant.

A 5,000-year-old rock painting from Spain shows a woman gathering honey.

Hunting and fishing
Before animals were domesticated, important high-protein foods were obtained by hunting and fishing. Hunting was mostly carried out by men. They developed tools, such as the bow, spear, and knife to help them hunt. They also trained animals, like dogs, to help them in hunting. Men in traditional societies still hunt today.

Gathering
In terms of human history, agriculture is a fairly recent development. It began in several different places (China, Mesopotamia, India, Meso-America, and others), some time after 10,000 BC. Before then (and in some traditional societies today), most food was obtained by gathering. Women and children were responsible for collecting plants, fruits, roots, insects, and small animals which they brought back to share with the group.

Fast food
Modern methods of preserving, processing, and packaging food, and hurried lifestyles, have led to the development of fast food. Frozen pizzas or even whole meals can be bought in supermarkets. Hamburgers and fries are available almost everywhere.

Desert-dwellers are skilled at finding water. This San man of the Kalahari Desert uses a reed to drink water from a tree trunk.

Preparing food
While some foods (fruits, nuts, vegetables), can be consumed raw, many others need to be cooked or processed in some way. In industrial societies most preliminary processing is done in factories. In traditional societies food is usually prepared or processed by the women. Without machinery, or with only very basic tools, this can be a time-consuming job.

Beverages
While people can survive for quite long periods of time without food, they can't survive for more than two or three days without water.

Food and religion
Many religions have rules about eating – from what kinds of food should be eaten and when, to how they should be prepared and served. Fasting (not eating) is also a religious practice. During the month of Ramadan, for example, Muslims abstain from taking food and drink during the daylight hours.

Ants are a delicious treat for many traditional peoples.

Food today
People in industrial societies consume foods from every corner of the globe. Without thinking, they open the fridge or cupboard and take out milk produced on distant farms, bananas from Ecuador, wine from France or Italy, and a wide variety of canned, frozen, or preserved foods and drinks from around the world. In the past (and among traditional peoples today), people produced their own food, or bought locally-grown products.

Variety of foods
Most human beings are omnivores, which means that they eat a bit of everything, including both meat and plant foods. However, not everybody will eat all the available foods. Sometimes for religious reasons (Muslims, for example, never eat pork), or for health or personal reasons, people make a choice among the foods available. Sometimes foods that are considered a delicacy in one country will be regarded with suspicion or disgust by the inhabitants of another.

Offerings of fruit and vegetables at a Japanese shrine.

Hunger
The number of hungry people in the world increases each year. The main cause of hunger is poverty; in countries where families can afford food they usually manage to buy enough to feed themselves, even when food is scarce. There is a huge difference between the amount of food consumed in rich countries (where people eat up to 40 percent more calories than they need) and poor countries. The World Health Organization estimates that each person needs about 2,500 calories each day to meet basic needs.

The map shows areas of the world and the average number of calories people consume each day.

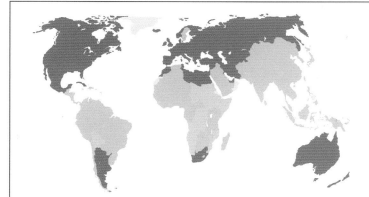

- ▮ Over 3,000
- ▮ 2,000-3,000
- ▮ Under 2,000

Inuit art

Traditional Inuit art includes carvings on bone, ivory, and stone. Modern artists continue this tradition, producing beautiful statues of human or animal figures. In recent years the name Inuit (meaning "the people") has been widely adopted instead of Eskimo, which some consider offensive.

Seal hunters

For traditional Inuit hunters, seals are a valued but difficult catch. Catching a seal means waiting long hours above a breathing hole until the animal comes up for air. When it does, the hunter has to move quickly to catch it before it disappears again. Every part of the animal is used. The fur makes warm clothing, the meat is eaten, and the bones are carved into useful tools.

Russian Orthodox priest blessing the fishing fleet on Kodiak Island.

Alaska

Aleuts, Inuit, and other Native American groups had been living in Alaska for thousands of years when the first European settlers arrived from Russia in the 18th century. In 1867 the United States bought Alaska from the Russian Government. It joined the Union on January 3, 1959. Some Russian traditions linger on in Alaska.

A Native American boy uses a net to catch salmon on Great Bear Lake.

The gold rush in Alaska

Many US citizens opposed the government when it bought Alaska. They only began to see Alaska's potential when gold was discovered towards the end of the 19th century.

A few people still search the remote valleys and rivers of Alaska and Canada for gold.

Salmon fishing

Salmon are common over much of Western Canada. Commercial fishing is an important activity.

Canada

The name Canada comes from a Huron-Iroquois word, Kanata, meaning village or settlement. Canada is the second largest country in the world, after Russia. More than 75 percent of all Canadians now live in urban centers. The main cities and most productive farmlands are concentrated in a narrow strip along the border with the United States. About 90 percent of the population lives in this area.

Totem poles, carved by the Indians of the Northwest coast, are decorated with animal figures.

Forestry

Almost a half of Canada's land area is covered with forest. Many people are employed in the lumber and related industries. Canada is a world leader in the export of pulp, paper, lumber, and other forest products.

Traditional arts and crafts are kept alive by a new generation of artists. Many live by selling their work to tourists.

Native Americans

When Europeans first arrived they found many different groups of Native American peoples. The Europeans took their land and spread diseases, greatly reducing the population. Today the Native American population is once again on the increase.

Language in Canada

In a recent survey 60 percent of Canadians said that English was their first language, while 24 percent named French as their mother tongue. Most of the remaining 16 percent speak other European languages, while a few recent immigrants speak Asian or Middle Eastern languages.

The Mounties

The Royal Canadian Mounted Police is Canada's federal police force. In the early days they did everything from helping settlers cope with the wilderness to patrolling the US border.

Canada, Alaska and Greenland

The earliest settlers of North America and Greenland came from Asia many thousands of years ago. They crossed a natural bridge of land and ice in the Bering Strait that linked present-day Siberia and Alaska. These first migrants journeyed south, probably following herds of bison, mammoth, and the other wild animals they hunted. They, and the many groups that followed, were the ancestors of today's Native Americans. Among the last to cross the Bering bridge before it disappeared were the Inuit peoples who settled the northernmost coasts of North America, and Greenland. About 1,000 years ago Viking explorers under Eric the Red settled in Greenland. Their farming villages thrived for about four centuries before dying out. The Vikings also visited Newfoundland in North America. European exploration began again at the end of the 15th century, but settlements were only established in Canada at the beginning of the 17th century. The English and the French fought for control of the vast territories of Canada. The English won in the end, but an active French culture remains to this day, particularly in the French-speaking province of Québec. Canada gained its independence from Britain in 1867, but is still a member of the Commonwealth. Today it is a wealthy, multicultural, modern democracy. Alaska is a part of the United States. Greenland is officially part of Denmark, although it achieved home rule in 1979.

Greenland girl on her birthday, opening gifts from family and friends.

Greenlanders today
Nearly four-fifths of modern Greenlanders are descendants of the first Inuit settlers. Most of the others are immigrant Danes from Denmark. Fishing and mining are the main economic activities and most people work in these industries.

Loading up the family snowmobile after a trip to the supermarket.

Getting around
Greenland has a cold Arctic climate. Snow and ice are normal conditions. Snowmobiles are widely used for transport.

Igloos
An igloo is a winter house made of blocks of ice. Nowadays most Inuit live in modern homes, but hunters in the far north still use them.

Inuit hunter builds an igloo as shelter from a storm.

The Vikings in North America
Although traditional Norse literature tells of Leif the Lucky's voyages to "Vinland", it wasn't until the 1960's that archeologists found proof that Vikings had visited North America.

Bronze pin of Norse origin found in northern Newfoundland.

The quest for independence
Over 80 percent of the population of Québec are of French origin and speak French. Many citizens of Québec would like to form their own independent state. A referendum was held in 1996. The decision to remain within Canada won, but by a very narrow margin and the question is by no means resolved.

Quebec City
The oldest city in Canada and the capital of the French province of Québec.

The Château Frontenac.

A woman of Caribbean origin dressed for the Caribana Festival held each summer in Toronto.

Immigration in Canada
Immigrants from Europe, Asia, Africa, and the rest of the American continent have joined the original mix of Native Americans, English, and French in Canada. Every year Canada accepts about 250,000 new arrivals from countries all over the world.

Traditional ways of life
In traditional Inuit society women cleaned and cured animal skins, made clothes, and cooked. The men hunted and carved tools and weapons from bone and ivory. Nowadays only a few people in the north live in traditional ways.

The United States of America

The area currently occupied by the United States was first inhabited about 30,000 years ago by people originally from Asia. These first peoples, now called Native Americans, spread out over the vast continent, giving rise to many nations, each with its own language, religious beliefs, and political and social structures. European explorers and traders came from the end of the 15th century. Two centuries later, the first European settlements were established by the English along the Atlantic coast. In the following centuries, wave upon wave of immigrants arrived from all over the world. The ever-increasing numbers of land-hungry farmers pushed the new country's frontiers westward to the Pacific. This process led to the near extinction of the Native Americans, who now make up less than one percent of the population. English is the official language in the USA today, although the immigrant communities, especially the latest arrivals, continue to speak their first languages. It is said that 100 languages are spoken in Los Angeles alone. Spanish is rapidly becoming the second language across the United States.

UNITED STATES OF AMERICA
Pop. (including Alaska and Hawaii) 268,700,000
Cap. Washington DC

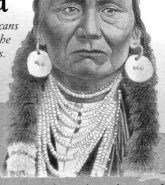

Columbus called Native Americans "Indians" because he thought he had reached the East Indies.

The "Indians"
Native American peoples are organized in tribes and groups of tribes, called nations. When Europeans first came to America there were four main groups: the farming communities of the East coast, the hunters of the Great Plains, the architects of the Southwest (who built the first towns), and the fishermen and hunters of the Pacific Northwest.

California is known for its high-tech and computer industries.

Virtual reality
California, on the West Coast, is called the "Golden State" after the gold found here in 1848. People have poured into the cities of Los Angeles, San Francisco, and San Diego in search of jobs, sunshine and the Californian "good life".

Agriculture
The USA is self-sufficient in food and even has some spare farm products for export. Huge farms, specialization, and high technology are responsible for the high output.

Country lifestyles and world views are very different from those in the big cities.

Hollywood, in Los Angeles, is the center of American film-making.

Native Americans
In the past, many Native Americans were forced off their lands and settled on reservations. The move from ancestral lands was devastating. The population dropped dramatically and Native Americans came to be known as the "Vanishing Americans". The situation has improved in recent years. From the 1960s onward, they have struggled to have their rights and cultures respected.

Navajo woman weaving at a traditional loom. The Navajo reservation in the Southwest is the largest in the country.

The American Dream
The USA is one the most culturally varied countries in the world. Over the last 500 years more than 60 million immigrants from almost every country in the world have made their homes here. The nation is based on the ideal of individual freedom and the belief that by working hard, all Americans can achieve material well-being, regardless of their origins. Not everybody would agree that this is actually true.

Entertainment
Americans take their leisure time seriously. The variety of entertainment in America is truly vast. Sporting events, movies, concerts, theater, television, amusement parks, restaurants, parties, barbecues, discos, and bars are just some of the most popular entertainments.

Immigration today
Although unlimited immigration was ended in the 1920s, the USA continues to accept about 500,000 immigrants each year. The majority of the newcomers are from Asia or Latin America. A large proportion of them settle in New York or other big cities. They often join family or community-based groups, which maintain the language and customs of their country of origin. Chinatown, in New York, has a foreign-born population of over 100,000.

Illegal immigration
Each year more immigrants enter the USA illegally than legally. Many come from Mexico and the rest of Latin America. Like all immigrants they come to seek a better life for themselves and their children. They often work in jobs the locals won't do, receiving low pay. They receive no welfare benefits and in many states are not accepted in hospitals or schools.

An Italian family arriving at Ellis Island in New York in 1900. Until the 1920s, 80 percent of all newcomers were inspected and processed on Ellis Island.

Sports and leisure

The most popular spectator sports, like baseball and basketball, have become a form of show business. Marching bands and cheerleaders are hired to attract and entertain. The big games are televised and watched by millions of fans across the nation.

Sports are the most popular form of recreation in the USA. Americans enjoy individual activities such as jogging, fishing, skiing, tennis, and hunting, as well as team sports, like baseball, basketball, and football. Most American schools have good sports facilities and children are encouraged to participate from an early age. Some students even earn sports scholarships to universities.

The President

The president of the USA is a very powerful person. The president, Congress, and the Supreme Court act together to govern the country.

Abraham Lincoln was president during the Civil War. He was assassinated just days after Union victory.

New telecommunication systems

Software producers have created a new way of communicating using traditional telephone lines. WWW, the World Wide Web, connects over 30 million computers. It allows people to exchange short or long, visual and/or audio messages across telephone lines.

America on wheels

The car has become a part of the American way of life. It is the most popular form of transport and there are over 150 million vehicles on the road. There are many drive-ins, and in some places you can shop, eat, go to the bank, see a film, go to church, or even attend a funeral, without ever getting out of your car.

The Ford Motor Company introduced the production line in Detroit in 1913. Prices dropped and for the first time owning a car was possible for ordinary people. By 1916 the Model T was selling at just $360 and over 15 million vehicles were sold.

Asian-Americans

In recent decades increasing numbers of Asians have settled in the USA. Many have been very successful in their new home.

Moving West

It is interesting to note that the states on the Eastern Seaboard generally have European names. Move West, as settlers did, and you encounter increasing numbers of American names, often based on Native American languages.

Some Native American state names and their meanings:
Dakota (Sioux) – "friend"
Mississippi (Chippewa) – "big river"
Kentucky (Iroquois) – "meadow land"
Idaho (Shoshone) – "light on the mountains"
Kansas (Sioux) – "land of the south wind people"

The new frontier

American space exploration culminated in 1969 when Apollo 11 took the first men to the moon. During the 1970s deep-space probes, such as *Viking* and *Voyager*, greatly enriched our knowledge of the outer planets of our solar system. Today, research is chiefly concentrated on the development of space shuttles.

A space shuttle is launched at Cape Canaveral in Florida.

Blues and jazz are a mixture of African and European music. They developed out of the spirituals and work songs of the African slaves as they worked in the fields.

Religious freedom

The birth of the United States is usually traced to the arrival of the English Pilgrims on the rocky Massachusetts coast, at a place named Plymouth. Many of the Pilgrims were Puritans, a Protestant group that had suffered persecution in England. Since then, many others have come to pursue their religious beliefs. Freedom of religion is guaranteed by the Constitution.

Puritan immigrant from England in the 17th century.

City life

Over 75 percent of all US citizens live in cities. Many of the large cities have high-rise buildings in the center which fill up during the day as commuters come to work. At night the commuters travel back home to the suburbs.

New York is the largest city in the USA. Over 18 million people live in greater New York.

Hasidic Jews (a sect of Judaism) often wear distinctive clothing. This young boy wears a traditional hat and "pais", unshorn locks of hair.

Most of the six million Jews in the USA today live in the large cities of the East Coast.

Jewish Americans

Since 1840 more than 3 million Jews have immigrated to the USA. The majority have come from Europe. Jewish immigrants, chiefly from Eastern Europe, are still arriving today.

African-Americans

Between 1620 and 1860, several million Africans were brought to America as slaves. Even after slavery was abolished in 1865, they still had to contend with segregation and discrimination. They lived in separate neighborhoods and attended separate schools. Many jobs were denied them and, especially in the South, whites tried to prevent them from voting. The civil rights movement of the 1950s and '60s, when many laws were passed to guarantee equality to Americans of all races, greatly improved the situation.

Mexican businessman.

A restive frontier

Two powerful cultures face each other across the long Mexican-US border. Each day thousands of people pass legally from one country to the other to work, shop, or visit friends or family. Others cross illegally from Mexico into the USA in search of work.

MEXICO
Pop. 97,100,000
Cap. Mexico City

BELIZE
Pop. 215,000
Cap. Belmopan

GUATEMALA
Pop. 10,900,000
Cap. Guatemala City

EL SALVADOR
Pop. 5,900,000
Cap. San Salvador

HONDURAS
Pop. 5,950,000
Cap. Tegucigalpa

NICARAGUA
Pop. 4,600,000
Cap. Managua

COSTA RICA
Pop. 3,420,000
Cap. San José

PANAMA
Pop. 2,700,000
Cap. Panama City

BAHAMAS
Pop. 300,000
Cap. Nassau

CUBA
Pop. 11,100,000
Cap. Havana

HAITI
Pop. 7,300,000
Cap. Port-au-Prince

PUERTO RICO
Pop. 3,670,000
Cap. San Juan

LESSER ANTILLES

DOMINICAN REPUBLIC
Pop. 7,900,000
Cap. Santo Domingo

JAMAICA
Pop. 2,530,000
Cap. Kingston

ST KITTS AND NEVIS
Pop. 43,000
Cap. Basseterre

ANTIGUA AND BARBUDA
Pop. 66,000
Cap. St John's

DOMINICA
Pop. 71,000
Cap. Roseau

ST LUCIA
Pop. 142,000
Cap. Castries

ST VINCENT AND THE GRENADINE
Pop. 112,000
Cap. Kingstown

BARBADOS
Pop. 262,000
Cap. Bridgetown

GRENADA
Pop. 92,000
Cap. St George's

TRINIDAD AND TOBAGO
Pop. 1,300,000
Cap. Port of Spain

Sumptuous dress

Tarahumara Indians live as farmers in northern Mexico. They wear stunning costumes during religious and seasonal fiestas.

Tarahumara ceremonial dress can include a small mirror in the elaborate headgear.

The People of Mexico

Mexicans are descendants of Amerindians and Spanish settlers. Over 90 percent of the population speaks Spanish. More than 5 million Amerindians continue to speak their native languages and many Mexicans are bilingual.

Maya descendants

The Lacandón people live in the tropical rain forest on the border between Mexico and Guatemala. They are direct descendants of the Mayans, whose great civilization flourished between 200 – 1500 AD. Today they live as farmers and hunters. Because of disease and assimilation, there are just a few hundred left.

Peyote rituals

While many Amerindians have converted to the Roman Catholic church, they continue to celebrate ancient rites and festivals. Some take the peyote cactus during religious ceremonies.

Huichol face painting for the peyote ceremony.

Nuestra Señora de Guadelupe, Mexico City.

Mexico City

Ciudad de México is one of the largest cities in the world. Around 20 million people, or about one-fifth of the population of Mexico, live there.

Huge stone head left b the Olmec people.

Maya pyramid-temple at Chichén Itza.

Central America

At least two-thirds of Central Americans are of mixed ethnic origins. Guatemala is the only country with a large Amerindian population. Most of the people live away from the coasts in the cooler, central highland regions. Birth rates are high and the population in most countries is increasing rapidly.

Lacandón youth in traditional white costume.

Nicaragua

Long years of civil war have greatly impoverished Nicaragua. As in many other Central American countries, a few people are very rich, while most of the others live in extreme poverty.

Farming family in Nicaragua.

Mexico and Central America

Central America is the narrow strip of land joining the countries of North and South America. Mexico lies to the north. The area stretches from the Mexican frontier with the United States to Panama's border with Colombia in the south. American Indians first settled here many thousands of years ago. Starting well over 1000 BC, these ancient peoples created a series of great civilizations, comparable to those of Mesopotamia and Ancient Egypt. They included the Olmecs, Mayas, Zapotecs, Teotihuacán, and Aztecs. They built great cities, invented writing and calendars, evolved complex religious, social, and political systems, and left outstanding examples of architecture, jewelry, and art. All this ended when the Spanish *conquistadores* arrived in the 16th century. They destroyed the Native American civilizations and, together with other European settlers from Holland, England, and France, took control of the entire region. They imported slaves from Africa and indentured workers from India and China. Today most Central American countries are free of their European colonizers. The majority of the people are of mixed ethnic origin. Spanish is the dominant language, although Amerindian and Carib languages, Creoles, English, and French are also widely spoken. Small minorities speak Hindi and Chinese. Christianity, mainly Roman Catholicism, is the most common religion.

Cuban cigars are famous the world over.

African Central Americans
European settlers brought people from Africa to work as slaves on their sugar and cotton plantations. When slavery ended, the Africans settled on the land or moved to the cities to live.

Tobacco
comes from the Americas. Before Europeans came, Native Americans smoked the rolled up leaves during ceremonies and because they thought it was good for their health.

Arawak Amerindian boy from Puerto Rico.

First peoples of the Caribbean islands
Few of the original Amerindian people survived the arrival of the Europeans. Those who did have mostly intermarried with Africans and Europeans.

The French West Indies
The inhabitants of Martinique and Guadaloupe are citizens of France.

European styles of dress are common throughout Central America.

Voodoo
Voodoo is the main religion in Haiti. It is a mixture of Roman Catholic and traditional African beliefs. Voodooists believe in spirits called *loa*. They have services with song, dance, drumming, prayer, and ritual sacrifice of animals.

Reggae music and dreadlocks also come from Jamaica.

Voodoo dance.

Rastafarians
Rastafarians believe that Ethiopia in Africa is their homeland. The movement began in Jamaica, where over 90 percent of the people are of African origin.

Cuna woman from Panama in traditional dress.

Panama
Panama is richer than the other countries of Central America because of the Panama Canal linking the Atlantic and Pacific oceans. It was opened in 1914. Men came from all over the world to help build it. Many stayed on and settled with their families in Panama.

Eastern South America

SURINAME
Pop. 423,000
Cap. Paramaribo

VENEZUELA
Pop. 22,300,000
Cap. Caracas

GUYANA
Pop. 835,000
Cap. Georgetown

FRENCH GUIANA
Pop. 147,000
Cap. Cayenne

BRAZIL
Pop. 166,800,000
Cap. Brasilia

PARAGUAY
Pop. 4,830,000
Cap. Asunción

The huge country of Brazil, occupying almost half the entire continent, dominates the eastern part of South America. Like the rest of the Americas, the area was settled about 30,000 years ago by various groups of Amerindians arriving from the north. They lived mainly in small tribal communities from the coast to the Andes Mountains until the arrival of the Europeans in the 16th and 17th centuries. It has been estimated that when the Europeans first set foot in South America, there were 50 million people living there. After just 100 years of contact, the population had fallen to about 5 million. The South Americans died mainly because they were not immune to the new diseases the foreigners carried, but also because of wars and genocide. The Portuguese took control of Brazil, making slaves of many Amerindians to work on their plantations. They also imported nearly 4 million Africans to work as slaves. The Dutch, English, Spanish, and French fought it out for control of the other countries. Today, the area is a melting-pot of different languages and peoples. Portuguese is the most widely spoken language, but hundreds of Amerindian languages and Creoles, as well as Dutch, Spanish, English, French, Hindi, Urdu, Japanese, and others are also spoken. The Roman Catholic religion is the most widely practiced, although primal religions still thrive among some Amerindian peoples.

Yanomami

The Yanomami people survive by hunting, gathering, and some simple agriculture. They live on the border between Brazil and Venezuela. The self-contained groups of about 100 people build their family homes together in a circle. Like many other traditional peoples, the Yanomami are in real danger of extinction.

The great river

The Amazon River (*Rio amazonas,* in Portuguese) flows 4,000 miles across northern Brazil, from the Andes Mountains to the Atlantic Ocean. It has over 1,000 tributaries. The river is a natural highway through the impenetrable Amazon forest.

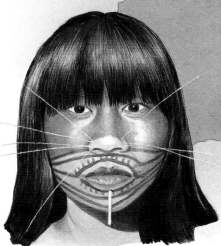

Amazonian peoples and reservations

Ever since Europeans arrived Amerindians have often been attacked and killed for their land. To help prevent confrontation, reservations have been created within the Amazon rain forest where they can live undisturbed. In some cases this has proved a satisfactory solution; in others, where the Amerindians have been forced to leave their lands, the pain has been so great that many have committed suicide or refused to continue their race by not having children.

The Matse - jaguar worshipers

The Matse people live in the west of the Amazon jungle, on the border between Brazil and Peru. Many still live traditional lives, the men hunting for meat while the women gather fruit, roots, and nuts. Many adults have a blue tattoo around their mouths and sticks in their lips and nose so that they look like jaguars. The Matse admire the stealth and beauty of the jaguar above all other animals.

Clearing the rain forest

The Amazon rain forest covers over 2.5 million square miles. It is the richest and most varied reserve of life on our planet. Several million species of plants, insects, birds, and other animals live there. But each year huge areas of the forest are cleared to make room for farmland and roads, and for forestry and mining operations. Scientists fear that extensive clearing may change our planet's climate.

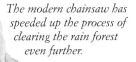

The modern chainsaw has speeded up the process of clearing the rain forest even further.

The Kamayura

The Kamayura people live in the Xingu National Park in central Brazil. They believe that a god created people from the bark of a tree. During the Kuarago festival, when they celebrate the creation of people, they play their long traditional flutes.

Yanomami man in festive dress visiting a neighboring village.

Wayana man and his son, of French Guiana.

From Venezuela to French Guiana

The countries of the northeast are inhabited by people of varied and mixed origins. There are many Asian Indians in Guyana and Suriname. Venezuelans are mainly of mixed European and Amerindian blood. People of African origin live throughout the area.

Carnivale!

Just before Lent every year a huge party takes place in the streets of Rio de Janeiro. It is called *Carnivale*, and for five days and nights the city is filled with colorful floats and people in stunning costumes dancing to samba music.

Brazilian woman in colorful carnival costume.

Body art

Every culture has its own idea of ideal beauty. The Poturù wear a wooden cylinder inserted in their bottom lip from the age of seven.

Shaman in ritual dance calls upon the spirits.

Caucciù

Some trees in the Amazon forest produce caucciù, a form of rubber used to make tires and shoes. To get at this valuable resource the government and private companies have often stolen the land from the tribes who live there, forcing them to move.

Shamanism

The shaman is an important figure in almost all Amazonian tribes. Usually a man, his main job is to heal people. But he is also called upon to divine future events, identify witches and other evil people, and help win wars. Most shaman use drugs to help them contact the spirit world.

Mineral wealth

Brazil has rich deposits of gold, iron, diamonds, nickel, and other minerals. These are precious resources for a developing nation, but miners are often made to work in dreadful conditions.

Candomblé

Candomblé is a religious cult based on a mixture of traditional African religions and Roman Catholicism. It is just one sect in the Afro-Brazilian Macumba religion. Candomblé is mainly practiced in the Bahia state in Brazil.

Vaqueiros – Brazilian cowboys

Until recently great herds of cattle grazed on open lands. They were herded by *vaqueiros*, or Brazilian cowboys. As farming methods change, they are gradually dying out.

What's cooking in Brazil?

Brazilian food is a mixture of all the cuisines of the country's inhabitants. *Feijoada,* made of rice, beans, meat, vegetables, and flour, is a typical dish.

Brazilian boy during initiation rites of a Candomblé sect.

Mennonites in Paraguay

Europeans have often sought religious freedom in the Americas. The Mennonites, a Protestant group of Dutch origin, have settled in Paraguay.

Street children

There are many *meninos da rua*, or "street children" in Brazil. They have no homes or families and must either beg or steal to survive.

Keeping cultural traditions alive

There is a tiny Japanese community in Brazil. They work hard at teaching their language and culture to their children.

Rich and poor

As in many other countries, the gap between rich and poor in Brazil is wide. Alongside the misery of the *favelas,* or shanty towns, there are wealthy modern suburbs where people lead pleasant lives.

Brazilian tea

Maté, a drink very similar to tea, is common in Brazil. In the past it was believed to hold magic powers and only shaman could drink it.

Western South America

The Andes Mountains stretch the length of western South America, from Colombia to Chile. Argentina backs onto the mountains in the south. The area was settled about 30,000 years ago. The early inhabitants cultivated crops, such as maize, peppers, squash, and potatoes. By 2500 BC there were thriving towns and ceremonial centers in what we now call Peru. Early civilizations, such as the Chavín, Moche, and Nazca, were succeeded in the 14th century by the Incas. Inca civilization was sophisticated, with extensive roads, irrigation, agriculture, mining, and a strong army, as well as complex social and religious organization. At its height, the Inca Empire stretched from modern Ecuador to central Chile. Its downfall began in 1532 when Francisco Pizarro, the first of the Spanish *conquistadores*, landed. The Europeans, hungry for gold, destroyed the Incas and other local populations, and gradually colonized the area with Spanish settlers. Exposure to new illnesses killed many of the Amerindians who had survived the conquest. Except for Argentina and Uruguay, the population of the region is now mainly *mestizo*, which means of mixed Spanish and Amerindian ancestry. Spanish is the official language in every country, and the Roman Catholic religion is predominant. All the countries in the area achieved independence from Spain in the 19th century. Many are still struggling with poverty, high inflation, and corrupt governments.

City life and country life
In Andean countries the cities have large groups of rich, well-educated people, usually of Spanish descent. The countryside is inhabited mainly by Amerindians who work in the mines or survive as subsistence farmers. Tension between the two groups sometimes explodes in episodes of violence.

Colombia
About 180 languages are spoken in Colombia. The Guajiro people live in northern Colombia. They are mainly nomadic herders.

Many Guajiro work in the salt mines for a part of the year. Women work as hard as the men, carrying huge sacks of salt.

Cocaine
Many farmers in Colombia grow the coca plant. The local people have always chewed coca leaves against illness and hunger. Now the plant is used to make the illegal drug, cocaine, which is exported to North America and Europe. Many farmers continue to grow coca plants because they are well paid.

Early civilizations
The central Andes were home to many civilizations before the Incas. The Chavín were the first to dominate the area. They were followed by the Moche, who have left us many fine examples of their skill as architects and artisans.

Gold and turquoise Moche ear ornament, about 300 AD.

Statue of an Inca god.

Lake Titicaca, the largest lake in South America.

Africans in the Andes
Africans were also brought to the Andes as slaves. Many of their descendants still live here today, particularly in Colombia and Ecuador.

Education
In recent years education has improved and the majority of children now have the opportunity to attend school. Almost all young people can read and write. School is taught in Spanish, which makes it harder for many Amerindian children who speak their own languages at home.

Schoolgirl in rural Ecuador. She rides for several hours each day to get to school.

In search of a better life
More and more people are moving from their country villages to the cities. Poor soil and lack of work make life in the country very hard. Small farmers pack up their belongings and walk to the nearest city in search of a job and a better life for their children. Often, however, they end up living in the huge slums that have grown up around many South American cities.

Aymara woman in Bolivia migrating to the city. She is wearing a traditional hat and polleras (layers of skirts, one over the other).

The Aymara people of Lake Titicaca
The Aymara live on the high plateau around Lake Titicaca in Bolivia and Peru. Despite the fact that they have been forced to live under first Inca and then Spanish domination, they have maintained their language and culture. Today they farm, fish, and raise livestock.

The Aymara build reed canoes which they use to navigate Lake Titicaca.

COLOMBIA
Pop. 38,300,000
Cap. Bogotá

ECUADOR
Pop. 11,460,000
Cap. Quito

PERU
Pop. 23,530,000
Cap. Lima

CHILE
Pop. 14,500,000
Cap. Santiago

BOLIVIA
Pop. 7,420,000
Cap. La Paz

URUGUAY
Pop. 3,190,000
Cap. Montevideo

ARGENTINA
Pop. 35,000,000
Cap. Buenos Aires

Argentina

Argentina differs from the Andean region because its population is almost entirely of European origin. Between 1850 and 1940 about three million Italians migrated to Argentina. Spanish, French, German, Portuguese, and other Europeans also came. By 1930, over 30 percent of the population was foreign-born.

South American cowboys

Raising stock is important in Chile and Argentina. In the past, cowboys (called *gauchos* in Argentina, and *huasos* in Chile), herded cattle in remote areas. They were admired for their courage, self-reliance, and love of the land.

Huasos in Chile.

Tango

The tango is a dance that originated in the poor suburbs of Buenos Aires towards the end of the 19th century. With its fast, sensual rhythms, at first it was considered scandalous. By the 1920s it was all the rage in Europe and North America. It was made even more famous by movie star Rudolph Valentino.

Population growth and urbanization

After the very fast rate of increase of recent decades, population growth is beginning to slow down. Cities are still growing very quickly, while fewer people live in the country. About 75 percent of all South Americans now live in cities.

Migrants

Spain began to colonize the Andean region and Argentina soon after the *Conquista* in the 16th century. However, it wasn't until the mid-19th century that settlers from Europe arrived in large numbers.

Chile

Chile is the longest country in the world. It stretches 2,700 miles down the west coast of South America. The original inhabitants, particularly the Mapuche people, fiercely resisted the Spanish conquest, although they lost in the end. Chile has rich forest, fishing, agricultural, and mineral resources.

Procession with the Virgin Mary.

Religion

The Spanish sent missionaries as well as soldiers and the population was soon converted to Christianity. Well over 90 percent of the population is still Catholic today. Sometimes local traditions and gods are worshiped alongside the Christian one. In Peru and Bolivia, for example, miners worship Tío, who represents both the Inca god of the Earth, and the Christian devil.

Machi during a ceremony to contact ancestral spirits.

Primal religion in Chile

Although Chile is a Catholic country, some traditional beliefs still exist. The Mapuche believe that misfortune, illness, and death are caused by evil magic. Healers, called machi, have special ceremonies to fight these evils.

Market days in the Andes are a chance to meet friends and catch up with local news. This young Chayas couple is dressed in traditional clothing for market day.

The original inhabitants

As on the rest of the continent, Amerindians suffered greatly from their first contacts with Europeans. Nevertheless, many indigenous cultures, religious beliefs, and languages have survived. The Quechua and Aymara languages of the Andean highlands are spoken by millions of people in Bolivia, Peru, Ecuador, and Colombia. In Bolivia, The Academy of the Aymara Language is dedicated to preserving the purity of that language. Quechua (along with Spanish) is the official language in Peru.

Folk festivals in the Andes

In the Andes, where the Amerindian population is large, folk festivals are a mix of local and Spanish tradition. The European invaders and their culture are often caricatured in dance and song.

Devil mask at the Oruro Festival in Bolivia.

Figure from an Ancient Greek vase. He is holding a lyre.

Art, Dance and Song

Art exists in all human societies. It is unique to humans. No other animal attributes value or beauty to an object it has created. The origins of art are unknown but, at some point in prehistory, people began to make and value items that were of religious or symbolic importance. Some of the oldest examples of "art", such as rounded female statues, rock paintings, and rows or circles of huge stones, were probably created for religious rites or ceremonies. Art and religion have been closely related ever since and many great works of art have been inspired by religion. Dance and song are also forms of art. We know that ancient peoples sang and danced because we have pictures of them doing so, although we don't know what their music sounded like.

Greek music

Ancient Greek philosophers thought that the study of music was an essential part of a good education. Greek music included vocals (often poems set to music), accompanied by a hand-held instrument.

Musical instruments

Musical instruments have been used since earliest times. They can accompany singing or dancing, religious ceremonies, work groups, or can be listened to on their own, for entertainment. For simplicity, the enormous variety of musical instruments can be divided into three basic groups: string (violin, cello), wind (oboe, clarinet), and percussion (piano, drum).

An elaborate Burmese harp.

Festivals

Among traditional peoples, religious or folk festivals often unite the entire spectrum of the arts, with music, dancing, theater and recitals, and specially created works of art for processions or to decorate the home and temple.

The Blues is a style of music created by African-Americans in the early part of the 20th century. Blues songs are often sad and tell about love gone wrong.

Song

Song was probably the first form of music. When early humans learned to talk, they also learned to sing.

Orchestral music

An orchestra consists of a group of musicians playing a variety of instruments together. In Western music, a typical orchestra combines string, wind, and percussion instruments. A full symphony orchestra can have as many as 50 string instruments accompanied by the same number of wind and percussion instruments. The orchestra is led by a conductor who keeps time and interprets the music. The conductor uses a baton, but he also uses his eyebrows, fierce glances, and often, his whole body, to encourage and lead the musicians.

The horse has a special place in Hindu mythology. It is believed that the god Vishnu will return as Kalkhi, riding on a white horse. He will slay all evil and re-establish pure religion. Vishnu's return is acted out on a beach in southern India.

Folk music

Many ethnic groups have their own typical music. It is learned by ear and handed down from generation to generation. Folk music is constantly changing and often contains something of the history and character of the people who play it. Many composers of classical music have been inspired by folk music.

A five-top metal drum from southern India. It is played during religious ceremonies.

Young people the world over are united by their love of dancing to the fast, exciting rhythms of pop and rock music. Concerts and discotheques are among the most popular forms of entertainment.

Dance

Dancing consists of moving the body in a rhythmic way to express an idea or a feeling, or simply to release excess energy. It is one of the oldest forms of art, and some type of dance exists in virtually every human society. Theatrical or classical dance is common in many countries. It consists of highly trained dancers performing a series of planned movements, usually for entertainment or religious purposes. Dance in tribal societies can be quite different. In many cases the dancers are not professionals and many members of the tribe take part. Tribal dances can be performed for a variety of reasons, including war, hunting, initiation, fertility rites, and worship. Other forms of dancing include folk dances and social dancing.

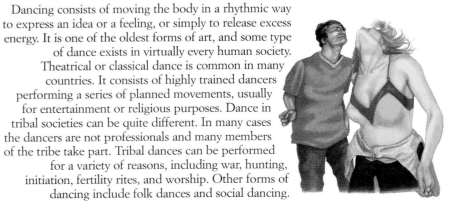

Quetzalcóatl, or the Plumed Serpent, shown here while eating a man, was one of the major gods in the ancient Mexican pantheon. In some pre-Colombian cultures, Quetzalcóatl was also represented as man. Many beautiful temples were built in his honor.

In Native American mythology the Thunderbird was a powerful spirit in the form of a bird. It was responsible for watering the earth. The flapping of its wings was thought to produce thunder, while lightening flashed out of its mouth. It was often shown with a second face on its stomach.

Representations of the Madonna became common in Western religious art after 431 when the Roman Catholic church established that Mary was the "Mother of God". She is often shown with the child Jesus in her arms.

Art and religion

Many of the greatest works of art and architecture were created for religious purposes. For example, the Parthenon in Athens, was built in honor of the goddess Athena; St. Peter's in Rome, and many other beautiful churches as well, were built in honor of the Christian god. The pre-Colombian cultures of Central America erected pyramids to their gods, while in India elaborate temples and statues celebrate Hindu divinities.

Art that tells a story

Many churches and religious buildings in Europe contain frescoes or works of art that were painted to help people understand an episode from the Bible or a special event in the life of a saint. Up until recently many ordinary people couldn't read and visual representations were an effective way for them to learn about religion.

Ukiyo-e

Ukiyo-e is a Japanese term which means 'pictures of the floating world'. It refers to the main artistic movement in Japan in the 17th to 19th centuries. Famous artists, such as Kitagawa Utamaro and Katsushika Hokusai, created prints portraying beautiful women or stars of *Kabuki* theater. When these prints first came to Europe in the 19th century, their flat decorative colors greatly influenced avant-garde artists, such as Claude Monet and Vincent Van Gogh.

Woman and child with a work basket, *a work by Kitagawa Utamaro (1753-1806).*

Indigenous art in Australia

Limestone engravings in a cave at Koonalda in South Australia have been dated to 20,000 years ago. Rock paintings in the Northern Territories are from about the same time. Aboriginal art today includes bark paintings, ritual objects, sculpture, body decorations, jewelry, and sand sculptures.

Traditionally, the Aboriginal art of Australia was created for religious beliefs and ceremonies. The figures and designs in the paintings have special meanings and each painting usually relates to a myth or tells a story. Some paintings use an "X-ray" technique which lets you see the heart, bones, or even a baby, inside the figure portrayed.

Art and medicine

Among the Navajo, Native Americans of the Southwest, dry-paintings were used in healing ceremonies. Helpers collected the materials, including sand, pollen, crushed flowers, charcoal, and colored sandstone, in the early morning. These were pulverized to create the five sacred colors of Navajo mythology – blue, black, white, red, and yellow. The powder was used to create a multicolored painting or design. The patient sat in the middle, facing east. Parts of the painting were sprinkled over him or her to draw out the evil, which was thought to be replaced by the good forces in the painting.

Navajo medicine man today creating a small dry-painting.

Movies

Movies are recognized as one of the most recent of the fine arts. They were invented in France in 1895 by the Lumière brothers. The first films with themes and actors were made at the beginning of the 20th century. They were silent and in black and white; sound was not introduced until 1926 and color until 1932. The talkies (as the first movies with a sound track were called) became extremely popular. Hollywood reached its zenith during the 1930s and early 40s. After World War II film studios in France, Italy, and the United Kingdom rose to prominence as well. Since the late 1970s, movies have become less popular (probably due to television) and the film industry has declined a little.

Some of the glamour and excitement of the film industry is kept alive today by film festivals and awards. The most famous of these are the Academy Awards ("Oscars") presented each year in Hollywood, and the annual festivals held at Cannes (France) and Venice (Italy).

The Berber people

The Berbers have lived here since ancient times. Despite numerous invasions they have retained much of their original culture. Berber dialects are still widely spoken.

A Berber girl dressed for her marriage.

The Tuareg wear blue turbans and veils to protect themselves from the desert sun. The dye stains their faces and they are often called Blue Men.

Women in Northern African countries

As in many Muslim societies, contradictions exist between traditional beliefs and customs and the influence of Western lifestyles. Nowadays many women have better access to education and more personal freedom.

Djenne was an important market town in the 11th century.

African kingdoms

Many influential kingdoms flourished in Northern Africa from 800-1900. Their wealth was based on trading gold, ivory, and iron. As the Islamic influence gradually filtered south some cities, like Djenne, also became important centers of Islamic studies.

The Great Mosque at Kairouan in Tunisia is the most important Muslim center of worship in Africa.

Religion in Northern Africa today

People in the states bordering the Mediterranean Sea are almost entirely Muslim. Further south, and in Egypt, there is a mixture of Muslim, Christian, and primal religions.

Water is a rare and precious resource in the Sahara. Where possible, it is carried from rivers, oases, and lakes to irrigate the desert.

Prehistoric rock drawings

Beautiful rock drawings were discovered last century at Tassili-n-Ajjer, in Algeria. Little is known about the people who created them. There are scenes of hunting and herding, as well as some geometrical designs.

The Sahara

The Sahara Desert is roughly the same size as the United States and is growing larger year by year. Only about 2.5 million people live here and they are either nomads or settled around the few oases.

The Blue Men of the desert

The Tuaregs are a Berber people. Once nomadic herders ranging across much of eastern North Africa, governments in the area have now curtailed their movements and fewer and fewer are able to lead traditional lives.

From traditional villages to modern metropolises

The number and variety of ways of life in Northern Africa is astounding. With more than 12 million inhabitants, Cairo, in Egypt, is a huge metropolis. Other African cities are also growing quickly as people move from rural areas to towns, and because the natural birth rate in Africa is relatively high. At the same time, many people continue to live in small villages in much the same way as their parents and grandparents did before them.

Building a home using traditional methods, in Niger.

WESTERN SAHARA
Pop. 190,000
Cap. Al-Aioun

ALGERIA
Pop. 29,800,000
Cap. Algiers

MOROCCO
Pop. 27,030,000
Cap. Rabat

TUNISIA
Pop. 8,890,000
Cap. Tunis

LIBYA
Pop. 5,400,000
Cap. Tripoli

EGYPT
Pop. 61,400,000
Cap. Cairo

ERITREA
Pop. 3,530,000
Cap. Asmera

DJIBOUTI
Pop. 570,000
Cap. Djibouti

SOMALIA
Pop. 9,250,000
Cap. Mogadiscio

MAURITANIA
Pop. 2,270,000
Cap. Nouakchott

NIGER
Pop. 9,150,000
Cap. Niamey

SUDAN
Pop. 28,090,000
Cap. Khartoum

MALI
Pop. 10,800,000
Cap. Bamako

CHAD
Pop. 6,360,000
Cap. Ndjamena

ETHIOPIA
Pop. 56,680,000
Cap. Addis Ababa

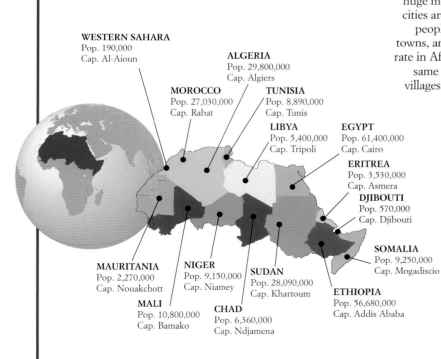

Beauty contests for men

The Wodaabe people celebrate the end of the rainy season with a festival called *Gerol*. The young men paint their faces, dress up in fancy clothes and parade before the women who choose the most beautiful from among them. The Wodaabe are part of the Muslim Fulani or Peul peoples of eastern and central Africa.

Northern Africa

Northern Africa is almost entirely covered by the Sahara, the largest desert in the world. Inhabited from earliest times, the history of this region is rich and varied. Ancient Egypt, one of the first great civilizations, developed along the banks of the Nile River. Later, further south, wealthy trading kingdoms flourished even into the 19th century. The Kanem-Bornu Empire, in Chad, was one of the most influential. Northern Africa has been invaded many times. The Islamic conquest in the 7th century changed the area more than any other. Even today, most of the people are Arab-speaking Muslims. Large pockets of indigenous Berber-speaking groups remain in Morocco and Algeria. During the 19th and 20th centuries France, England, Italy, and Spain colonized the countries of Northern Africa. Although the colonial era is now over, European influence has had a lasting effect on the languages spoken, culture, and the artificial national boundaries that were imposed. Boundary disputes have led to frequent conflict. Poverty, harsh climatic conditions, religious intolerance, and warfare continue to plague many countries in the region.

The Bedouin
The Bedouin are an Arabic-speaking people of the deserts of eastern North Africa and Arabia. Originally nomadic herders, many have been forced to settle in towns and cities in recent years.

The jelaba
The striped cotton *jelaba* is worn by men and boys throughout North Africa.

The Chepren Pyramid, famous for its sphinx, dates from 2588 BC.

Ancient Egypt
The first great African civilization grew up 5,000 years ago in the fertile Nile River Valley. Ancient Egyptians knew how to build huge pyramids and tombs, they had a written language, and a sophisticated society and religious beliefs.

The Ethiopian Orthodox Church
Ethiopia is the only country in Northern Africa where most people are Christians. Ethiopia was Christianized in the 4th century. Some traditional beliefs and spirits have been incorporated into the Christian doctrine.

Priest during the Maskal (Cross Festival).

The burda
Among the Rashaida, a Muslim people of Sudan and Ethiopia, the traditional Muslim face veil is called a *burda*. All women over the age of four must wear the veil, which reaches to the ground. They never take it off, even when they eat.

The Dinka
The Dinka are a pastoral people of the Upper Nile Valley. Many of them still lead traditional lives. They wear tight-fitting corsets, the colors of which change according to the age of the wearer. They are red and black from 15 to 25; red and purple from 25 to 30; and yellow from 30 and over.

Surma girl with painted face.

Body painting
In the mountains of Ethiopia the Surma people paint and adorn their bodies as they have always done. The men decorate themselves with chalk-and-water designs. The women paint their faces and breasts. They also wear lip and ear plates.

Fighting infant mortality
Many African governments are trying hard to stop their children dying of disease and malnutrition. With the help of international aid organizations, millions of children have been vaccinated and fed.

A government worker helps a Maji mother weigh her baby in Ethiopia.

Peoples of the Upper Nile Valley
Many ethnic groups in the Upper Nile Valley live as herders. Their cattle are not only their main source of food, but also their only form of wealth. Cows are considered sacred.

Islam and Christianity

Islam and Christianity have nearly supplanted the traditional religions practiced in Central Africa. They were brought to the region by traders and missionaries.

Senegalese boy learning about Islam. Over 90 percent of the population of Senegal is Muslim.

Fort on the coast where Africans were held until a ship came to take them to America as slaves.

Slaves from Africa

Between the 16th-19th centuries, more than 12 million Africans were transported to the Americas as slaves. Many millions more are thought to have died during the long sea voyage from Africa because of the dreadful conditions on board the slave ships.

Colonialism and its aftermath

The colonial powers created countries in Africa with no regard for the traditional boundaries of the peoples who lived there. When the Europeans left, in many cases fighting broke out among groups who had nothing in common and who may have been enemies historically.

Bronze head of a royal person from Benin.

The elephant is the national symbol of the Ivory Coast.

Gold

Gold is an important resource in West Africa. The Akan, one of the many ethnic groups in the region, think of gold as a ground-dwelling spirit.

Ashanti man from Ghana sending a message by drums.

Traditional beliefs

A large number of Central Africans continue to follow traditional beliefs which have been handed down for centuries. Ancestors are an important part of these primal religions. Magic is another key element. Some individuals are believed to have special powers to contact ancestors and spirits, so that they can, among other things, cure illness, inhibit "bad" magic, and ensure the success of crops.

Farming

Maize, millet, sorghum, yams, and taro are among the main crops grown. Farming tends to be small scale, with production for the family group. Surplus products are sold or exchanged in village markets. The most important export items are cocoa, coffee, and cotton. In many areas women are mainly responsible for farming.

Woman in Nigeria winnowing grain which she will then grind and make into a local form of bread.

Only Bobo men are allowed to wear the masks.

Bobo masks

The Bobo people of Burkina Faso have hundreds of different colored masks which they use in ceremonies during the "season of the masks" from March to August. Each mask represents a mythical being or animal and each has its own story and purpose.

Language in Central Africa

Hundreds of different languages are spoken. Many people are bilingual, speaking one or more of the local tongues, plus one of the colonial languages (English, French, Portuguese), which are used as official languages in some countries.

Pile-dwelling in the swamp areas of Benin.

Markets

Market day in rural villages is the most important day of the week. The rhythm of life is measured by market day, thus a "week" might consist of 4 or 5 days, or the number of days from one market till the next.

In many areas, women control the markets, selling and exchanging the results of their labor at home or in the fields.

The bush telegraph

For thousands of years the beating of drums was the most effective way of communicating with people at a distance. In some remote areas the "bush telegraph" is still used today.

Tradition and change

Most people in Central Africa live in the country, either as settled farming peoples in small tribal villages, or as nomadic herders, or hunters and gatherers. Most belong to small, distinct and culturally diverse ethnic groups, each of which has its own traditions and language. This situation is changing gradually as people, usually young men, move to the cities in search of paid labor. Once settled, they send for their wives and children and other family members. The population of many cities in Central Africa has increased dramatically in recent years.

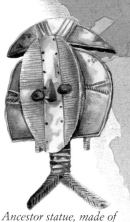

Ancestor statue, made of wood and human bones.

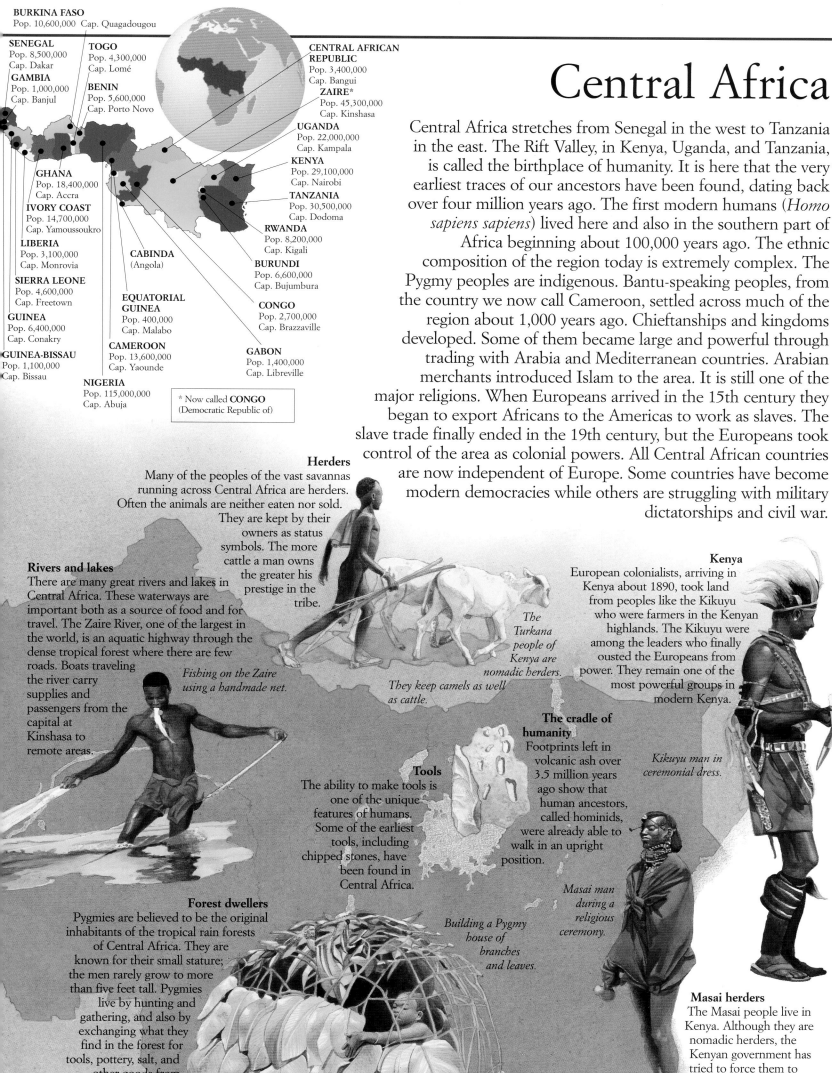

BURKINA FASO
Pop. 10,600,000 Cap. Quagadougou

SENEGAL
Pop. 8,500,000
Cap. Dakar

GAMBIA
Pop. 1,000,000
Cap. Banjul

TOGO
Pop. 4,300,000
Cap. Lomé

BENIN
Pop. 5,600,000
Cap. Porto Novo

GHANA
Pop. 18,400,000
Cap. Accra

IVORY COAST
Pop. 14,700,000
Cap. Yamoussoukro

LIBERIA
Pop. 3,100,000
Cap. Monrovia

SIERRA LEONE
Pop. 4,600,000
Cap. Freetown

GUINEA
Pop. 6,400,000
Cap. Conakry

GUINEA-BISSAU
Pop. 1,100,000
Cap. Bissau

NIGERIA
Pop. 115,000,000
Cap. Abuja

CABINDA
(Angola)

EQUATORIAL GUINEA
Pop. 400,000
Cap. Malabo

CAMEROON
Pop. 13,600,000
Cap. Yaounde

CENTRAL AFRICAN REPUBLIC
Pop. 3,400,000
Cap. Bangui

ZAIRE*
Pop. 45,300,000
Cap. Kinshasa

UGANDA
Pop. 22,000,000
Cap. Kampala

KENYA
Pop. 29,100,000
Cap. Nairobi

TANZANIA
Pop. 30,500,000
Cap. Dodoma

RWANDA
Pop. 8,200,000
Cap. Kigali

BURUNDI
Pop. 6,600,000
Cap. Bujumbura

CONGO
Pop. 2,700,000
Cap. Brazzaville

GABON
Pop. 1,400,000
Cap. Libreville

* Now called **CONGO** (Democratic Republic of)

Central Africa

Central Africa stretches from Senegal in the west to Tanzania in the east. The Rift Valley, in Kenya, Uganda, and Tanzania, is called the birthplace of humanity. It is here that the very earliest traces of our ancestors have been found, dating back over four million years ago. The first modern humans (*Homo sapiens sapiens*) lived here and also in the southern part of Africa beginning about 100,000 years ago. The ethnic composition of the region today is extremely complex. The Pygmy peoples are indigenous. Bantu-speaking peoples, from the country we now call Cameroon, settled across much of the region about 1,000 years ago. Chieftanships and kingdoms developed. Some of them became large and powerful through trading with Arabia and Mediterranean countries. Arabian merchants introduced Islam to the area. It is still one of the major religions. When Europeans arrived in the 15th century they began to export Africans to the Americas to work as slaves. The slave trade finally ended in the 19th century, but the Europeans took control of the area as colonial powers. All Central African countries are now independent of Europe. Some countries have become modern democracies while others are struggling with military dictatorships and civil war.

Herders
Many of the peoples of the vast savannas running across Central Africa are herders. Often the animals are neither eaten nor sold. They are kept by their owners as status symbols. The more cattle a man owns the greater his prestige in the tribe.

The Turkana people of Kenya are nomadic herders. They keep camels as well as cattle.

Rivers and lakes
There are many great rivers and lakes in Central Africa. These waterways are important both as a source of food and for travel. The Zaire River, one of the largest in the world, is an aquatic highway through the dense tropical forest where there are few roads. Boats traveling the river carry supplies and passengers from the capital at Kinshasa to remote areas.

Fishing on the Zaire using a handmade net.

Kenya
European colonialists, arriving in Kenya about 1890, took land from peoples like the Kikuyu who were farmers in the Kenyan highlands. The Kikuyu were among the leaders who finally ousted the Europeans from power. They remain one of the most powerful groups in modern Kenya.

Kikuyu man in ceremonial dress.

The cradle of humanity
Footprints left in volcanic ash over 3.5 million years ago show that human ancestors, called hominids, were already able to walk in an upright position.

Tools
The ability to make tools is one of the unique features of humans. Some of the earliest tools, including chipped stones, have been found in Central Africa.

Masai man during a religious ceremony.

Forest dwellers
Pygmies are believed to be the original inhabitants of the tropical rain forests of Central Africa. They are known for their small stature; the men rarely grow to more than five feet tall. Pygmies live by hunting and gathering, and also by exchanging what they find in the forest for tools, pottery, salt, and other goods from neighboring farmers.

Building a Pygmy house of branches and leaves.

Masai herders
The Masai people live in Kenya. Although they are nomadic herders, the Kenyan government has tried to force them to settle. Most Masai have refused and maintain their roaming ways.

Masks
Masks represent a spirit in village or tribal life. They are worn by a dancer who becomes the spirit and through the mask talks with villagers about important events, such as death, birth, marriage, or initiation.

Kalelwa mask from Angola used during initiation rites.

Zulu diviner or "Inyanga".

A woman in Zambia uses a mortar and pestle to grind millet.

A land of farmers
The majority of Southern Africans live by growing crops to eat and sell. They live traditional lives in country villages. Even so, this is changing fast as more and more people move to towns and cities in search of paid labor.

The struggle for power
After 400 years as a colony, Angola became independent from Portugal in 1975. Civil war followed as two political factions fought for power. The war has continued off and on ever since with devastating effects on the lives of most Angolans.

Angolan leader.

Ancestor worship
In traditional religions ancestors are believed to protect the living from sickness and trouble. They are worshiped with gifts and rituals. Diviners are people thought to have special powers who tell the people what the ancestors want.

Malawian girl.

Malawi
Malawi means "land lake where the sun is reflected in the water like fire". Most people live by farming and fishing in Lake Malawi.

First peoples
The San and Khoikhoin peoples have been living on the plains of Southern Africa for at least 10,000 years. Today only a few still live traditionally as hunters and gatherers of nuts, fruit and berries.

Fishing
Fishing is an important activity along the coasts and in the rivers and lakes throughout Southern Africa.

Herera woman in Namibia.

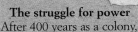

San Bushman elder.

Colorful costume
The Ndebele peoples in South Africa traditionally wore colorful costumes and beaded jewelry.

Ndebele woman in traditional dress.

Namibia, newly independent
Namibia gained independence from South Africa in 1990.

Miner in South Africa.

Settlers in South Africa
Over the centuries European and Asian peoples have settled in South Africa. The main groups are Dutch, English, and Indian. There are now four official languages: Afrikaans, English, Xhosa, and Zulu.

South African girl of Indian descent.

South African girl of Dutch descent.

Zulu necklaces.

Mozambique: a woman carries fish in a wooden basket on her head.

Women's roles
Over much of Southern Africa women are left behind in rural villages to manage homes, look after children, farm the land, and sell produce. The men move to the cities and mines for paid work.

Migrant labor
South Africa has a large mining industry which attracts men from all over the region. Many leave their families behind and move to the mines where they can earn relatively high wages. They send money home, but can often only visit two or three times a year.

Southern Africa and Madagascar

ZAMBIA
Pop. 9,700,000
Cap. Lusaka

ANGOLA
Pop. 11,500,000
Cap. Luanda

NAMIBIA
Pop. 1,600,000
Cap. Windhoek

BOTSWANA
Pop. 1,500,000
Cap. Gaborone

SOUTH AFRICA
Pop. 42,400,000
Cap. Pretoria

LESOTHO
Pop. 2,100,000
Cap. Maseru

ZIMBABWE
Pop. 11,500,000
Cap. Harare

SWAZILAND
Pop. 900,000
Cap. Mbabane

MADAGASCAR
Pop. 15,200,000
Cap. Antananarivo

MOZAMBIQUE
Pop. 16,500,000
Cap. Maputo

MALAWI
Pop. 11,400,000
Cap. Lilongwe

Khoisan peoples, including the San (or "Bushmen"), and the Khoikhoin, were the original inhabitants of Southern Africa. They speak unique click languages, so-called for the "clicking" sounds they use in speech. About 2,000 years ago Bantu-speaking ethnic groups from the north settled across the area. The vast majority of Southern Africans today are descendants of these Bantu and Khoisan peoples. From the 16th century onwards European explorers came. Mainly Portuguese, Dutch, English, and German, they settled on the land and mined for the immense mineral wealth in the region. In many countries they took over the government, often introducing racist forms of political control, such as the apartheid system in South Africa. Today, all the countries in the area are free of European colonial powers, although two, Angola and Mozambique, have had almost continual civil war since gaining independence in 1975. South Africa is the richest country. Its industry and mining attracts workers from rural areas and surrounding countries. Like the rest of Africa, the population is growing quickly. In most countries over half the population is under 15 years of age. Traditional African religions are observed and Christianity, introduced by the Europeans, is also widely practiced. Some countries have large Muslim communities.

Malagasy boy.

Madagasacar
The huge island of Madagascar was once joined to Africa. It detached itself about 170 million years ago and began drifting east.

Language
Like the people, the language of Madagascar is called Malagasy. French is also spoken, and both languages are taught in schools.

Outrigger canoe.

Ethnic groups
Madagascar was uninhabited until about 1,500 years ago, when people from far-off Indonesia came in outrigger canoes. Some settlers also came from Africa. Today, their descendants are known as Malagasy.

Tomb statue of a zebu (a kind of ox) being sacrificed.

Religion
About half the Malagasy are Christians. Most of the others follow their local religion, which is based on ancestor worship. Traditional Malagasy tombs are decorated with carved wooden statues showing events from the dead person's life.

The end of apartheid in South Africa
Apartheid, which means "apartness", was introduced in South Africa in 1948. It was a racist political system that kept ethnic groups separate and discriminated in favor of the small white minority. Black Africans were deprived of their political rights and most of their land, and many were sent to live on remote "home-lands." The long struggle by freedom fighters, together with international pressure, gradually wore the system down and in April 1994 the entire adult population went to the polls to elect a new multi-racial government. Nelson Mandela, veteran leader of the African National Congress, was elected president and a new constitution was written by representatives of all sectors of the community. The country's new national anthem is called *Nkosi Sikelel iAfrika* (God Bless Africa).

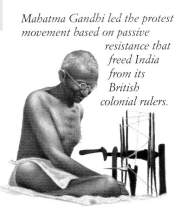

Cultures in Contact

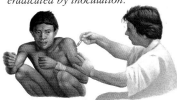

The meeting of two different ethnic groups always leads to an exchange of ideas, technology, and culture. This can be an invigorating experience for both, enriching and improving their traditional ways. However, if one of the groups presumes itself superior to the other, conquest and oppression occurs. History is full of examples of migrating peoples or invading armies who impose their religions, languages, and ways on peoples who either assimilate (accept the new ways), die out, or withdraw to the sidelines of history. There are many examples today of both successful and oppressive contact between cultures. The plight of indigenous peoples around the globe highlights many aspects of unsuccessful contact. The successes of some multicultural schools and communities are examples of positive contact.

Working together
Poverty, disease, and illiteracy continue in many parts of the world. However, much has been achieved in the last 50 years: infant mortality has been halved; the number of children starting school in the developing world has risen to 75 percent; average life expectancy has risen by one third. Many of these achievements are due to international organizations, such as the United Nations, working with local governments.

Conquest and colonialism
Beginning about 1500, the European nations of England, France, Germany, Portugal, the Netherlands, and Spain, conquered and settled large areas of the Americas, the Pacific, Asia, and Africa. Colonialism was almost always devastating for the original inhabitants of these regions. New religions and languages were introduced, often by force. Old ways were forbidden or looked down upon. Land was taken and sold to individuals, instead of being held communally. Sometimes indigenous peoples were simply massacred. In some countries, such as Canada or Australia, Europeans have remained and taken control of the country. In many others, such as India, the colonial power was expelled.

An Apache girl at an inter-tribal ceremony organized to celebrate and preserve Native American heritage.

Indigenous peoples in North America
More than half the 2 million Native Americans now live in cities, far from reservations. Community organizations, known as Indian Centers, provide health and social services, as well as much needed cultural support. The centers preserve Native American culture by organizing tribal ceremonies, and teaching the languages, songs, dance, and ways of life to new generations.

The National Museum of the American Indian
There are almost one million objects in the museum's collection. Many will be on display in a new museum in Washington, DC opening in the year 2000.

Indigenous peoples of Africa
Over the centuries, Arab invasions, the Muslim religion, European colonialism, Christianity, the slave trade, and, today, the influence of the modern world, have modified or extinguished many indigenous cultures. Even so, the variety of traditional peoples in Africa today is greater than in any other part of the world. In rural areas, many groups continue to lead lives in which indigenous knowledge, institutions, beliefs, and values are the primary source of life.

Fighting back
In the past some observers thought that all indigenous peoples would either assimilate or die out but recent developments have proved them wrong. Many groups reached a low point in the early decades of the 20th century, but since then their numbers have increased. Indigenous groups have organized to preserve their cultures and pass them on to their children. They also continue to fight oppressive groups and governments so they may be left in peace to live as they please.

The Cágaba people live in Colombia. They have a very rich tradition of folk tales, populated by supernatural beings. Some spirits are good and help humans, while others torment them.

The return of spring in Nepal is celebrated by a fertility dance. This masked dancer is believed to accompany Mother Earth when she descends to fertilize the soil, assuring plentiful crops in the coming year.

Indigenous peoples in the New World
Throughout the New World, the main killer after contact with Europeans was disease – influenza, measles, smallpox, diphtheria, and others. Disease and many problems caused by colonization, such as suicide, alcoholism, and drug abuse are still taking their toll today.

Spring 1816: the Tarabucos people of the Andes defeat the Spanish regiment "Los Verdes" in battle. According to legend, they cut the dead soldiers open and ate their hearts. Since then, they have worn a leather imitation of the Spanish helmet as part of their traditional costume.

Art thieves?

The museums of Europe and North America are full of stunning works of art from around the world. Many pieces were rightfully bought from their artists or owners. Others were taken during wars or invasions, or collected by travelers in foreign lands. Some people feel that many pieces should be returned to their countries of origin.

This statue, called a caryatid, comes from the Acropolis in Athens, Greece. It was taken to England by Lord Elgin almost 200 years ago and is now on display in the British Museum. The Greek government would like to have it back because it sees it is a symbol of Greece. The British would like to keep it, because they feel it is well looked after and on show for millions of people to enjoy.

Indigenous peoples of the North

The northern rim of the world is inhabited by a mosaic of hunter, gatherer, fisher, and herding peoples, many of whom have maintained traditional lifestyles up until today. The harsh climatic conditions and inhospitable natural environment of the far north discouraged settlement by other peoples. Recent discoveries of mineral resources are changing this.

The Chukchi people live in the tundra and along the coast of northeastern Siberia. They are reindeer herders, and hunters and fishermen.

Positive contact

Many European artists have been influenced and inspired by the art and cultures of other societies from around the globe.

French artist, Paul Gauguin, painted his greatest works while living in Polynesia, in the Pacific Islands. The local influence is clearly visible in these works. This figure comes from a famous painting called Woman Holding a Fruit (Where are you Going?).

This Ge girl's red cap in her headdress shows that she is unmarried. Ge girls spend years sewing elaborate costumes to demonstrate their skills to future husbands. The 70,000 Ge people live in the mountains of the Guizhou Province in southern China. In some Ge villages the day begins with a prayer to save the trees — they are a precious local resource.

Nomads have always lived in North and East Africa, the Arabian peninsula, Central Asia, and Siberia.

Disappearing nomads

Our word "nomad" comes from the Greek *nemein*, which means "roving for pasture". Nomads keep animals which they graze by moving continuously. In recent years, many of their traditional grazing lands have been taken by farmers. In other cases, their grazing lands have been limited by new national borders, or simply forced to settle by unsympathetic governments. The nomadic way of life is slowing dying out.

Indigenous peoples of Asia

More than half the indigenous peoples of the world live in Asia. Many are in China, where they suffered greatly during the "Cultural Revolution" of the 1960s and '70s. China now claims to pursue a more lenient policy, although it is still trying to assimilate indigenous populations. People of the forests of Asia, such as the Sarawak in Malaysia, are threatened by the lumber industry. In India too, indigenous people are relocated when the government wants to build a dam or log a forest.

The Elmolo people live on the shores of Lake Turkana, in Central Africa. Composed of about 40 individuals, they are one of the smallest ethnic groups in existence. If they are allowed to die out, yet another unique culture will disappear without a trace.

Indigenous peoples of Oceania

Indigenous peoples in Oceania include the Aborigines of Australia, the Polynesians of New Zealand and the Pacific, and Melanesian and Micronesian peoples in New Guinea and the Pacific. A strong desire for respect and recognition of their native cultures has led to many groups winning back rights to their ancestral lands and a rebirth of pride in indigenous languages and customs.

Long-distance hunting trips in the Kalahari are made easier when traveling on a bicycle.

This Aranda hunter in Australia is re-enacting an ancient myth. It tells the story of how his ancestors struggled with and killed two man-eating eagles that threatened the tribe. He is covered in eagles' feathers and the leaves he holds represent the bird's wings. The Aranda live in central Australia. Like other Aborigines, their numbers were greatly reduced after contact with Europeans, but the population is now increasing again. Some Aranda groups have won back their lands from the Australian government.

Sacred masks

In New Guinea and many of the surrounding islands masks are thought to represent spirits of dead ancestors and are used during funeral rites. They also appear during initiation ceremonies, when young adults are officially accepted into the adult community.

New Guinea

Irian Jaya has been a part of Indonesia since 1963. Papua gained its independence from Britain in 1975. It is a full member of the Commonwealth. Mining and agriculture are important for both countries. Attempts are being made to encourage tourism.

Languages

in New Guinea Over 700 different languages are spoken in New Guinea and its island neighbors.

Long distance learning

In the Australian outback distances are so great that children can't travel to school each day. They get lessons via radio or computer and learn at home.

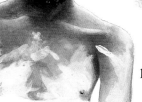

Farming in Australia

Sheep and cattle raising are important for the Australian economy. Many farms are huge and far from their neighbors. Farming families live isolated lives or travel enormous distances by plane or car to see other people.

The boomerang

The Aborigines used boomerangs for hunting and warfare. A few boomerangs are curved in shape and, if thrown properly, will complete a large circle before landing back at the thrower's feet.

Bark painting

The tradition of painting on eucalyptus bark still flourishes in many parts of northern Australia.

Mother and son spend Christmas day on the beach near Perth.

Body painting

Decorating the body is an essential part of the preparation for many Aboriginal rituals.

Australia – land of immigrants

Aborigines account for less than 2 percent of the population of Australia. The majority of the others are of British or Irish origin. After World War II Australia began to accept more non-British Europeans (mainly Greeks and Italians). Since the 1970's immigrants from many other parts of the world, but particularly from Asia, have also been admitted. Australia continues to accept about 12,000 refugees each year.

Italian-born immigrant in Melbourne.

Leisure time

The mild Australian climate encourages outdoor activities. Cricket, tennis, rugby, soccer, and horse-racing are very popular. Going to the beach is a national pastime.

After almost dying out early in the 20th century, the Aboriginal population is now on the increase again.

The Dreaming

Traditionally the Aborigines believed that the world about them, including themselves, their culture, and the physical landscape, was created by magical beings who emerged from the Earth during the Dreamtime. The Aborigines' duty was to take care of the world the spirits had created, keeping everything as it was and obeying the Dreaming rules. Many special rituals were carried out regularly to ensure continual contact with the spirits.

Forced immigration

Many of Australia's first European settlers did not choose to come to the colony. They were men and women who had been convicted of crimes in Britain or Ireland and were sent to Australia as punishment. After serving their sentences most stayed on and spent the rest of their lives in Australia.

Australasia

Australasia is composed of the South Pacific lands of Australia, New Zealand, and Papua New Guinea. Australia and Papua have been inhabited for about 50,000 years by people who came from Southeast Asia. Native Australian peoples, called Aborigines by English settlers, lived as food gatherers and hunters until extensive European settlement destroyed their traditional lifestyles. They had a deeply spiritual culture, expressed through complex myths and ceremonies. The first peoples of Papua raised pigs and grew crops. New Zealand lay uninhabited until about 800 years ago when a Polynesian people, called Maoris, settled there. They lived as hunters and farmers. During the 18th and 19th centuries Australia and New Zealand were settled by large numbers of Europeans, mainly from Great Britain and Ireland. The Aborigines and Maoris lost most of their land to the Europeans. Both populations were nearly destroyed by contact with European diseases to which they had no immunity. Today Australia and New Zealand both have developed economies and high living standards.

The island of New Guinea is divided into two parts, the western half, called Irian Jaya, is a part of Indonesia and is governed from Jakarta. The eastern half, called Papua New Guinea, is an independent country. English is the most common language in Australia and New Zealand. Christianity, mainly Protestantism, is the main religion, although some indigenous religions are practiced in Papua.

PAPUA NEW GUINEA
Pop. 4,070,000
Cap. Port Moresby

AUSTRALIA
Pop. 18,500,000
Cap. Canberra

NEW ZEALAND
Pop. 3,660,000
Cap. Wellington

Mbis pole

The Asmat people of Irian Jaya believed that death was not natural but always caused by an enemy. When a number of people in a village died, the survivors would hold a *mbis* ceremony. Special carvings were made, including *mbis* poles. The poles were placed in front of the men's ceremonial house. They stayed there until the deaths had been revenged by killing enemies. The heads of the dead were placed in the *mbis* poles, and later thrown away in the jungle.

Tourism

More and more people from all over the world are spending their holidays in New Zealand. An outdoor lifestyle, hiking, sailing, fishing, skiing, and unspoiled scenery and beaches are just a few of the attractions.

New Zealanders today

New Zealanders (often called Kiwis after the unique flightless bird that has been adopted as a national symbol), are mainly of British origin. About ten percent of the population is Maori, and there are also small groups of Pacific Islanders, Chinese, and Indians.

Traditional Maori greeting includes touching and rubbing noses.

Wood carving is a traditional Maori art. Elaborately decorated meeting houses provide a center for Maori reunions.

City dwellers

Although agriculture is still very important for the New Zealand economy, the great majority of the people live in towns and cities. About three-quarters of the population live in the North Island. The beautiful South Island remains more peaceful and rural.

The shearing season is one the busiest times of year on a New Zealand sheep farm.

Keeping Maori traditions alive

In recent years Maori people have tried to maintain and revive their traditional culture. They have organized groups to provide Maori language and culture lessons for children, and have tried to teach both young Maoris and *pakehas* (white New Zealanders) respect for their ways of life.

The Pacific Islands

The Pacific Ocean is the largest ocean, covering almost a third of the surface of our planet. A great variety of peoples live on the thousands of islands scattered across the Pacific. Traditionally, the region is divided into three areas – Melanesia, Micronesia, and Polynesia. Melanesia (including New Guinea) was settled first, about 50,000 years ago. Micronesia and Polynesia were settled by peoples from Melanesia about 3,000 years ago. When European explorers arrived in the 16th and 17th centuries, they found farming communities who grew vegetables and fruit and kept pigs, dogs, and chickens. In the 19th century almost all the islands passed under control of European powers and the United States. The majority of people were converted to Christianity by missionaries. Many of the Islands have now obtained independence from Europe and the US. Most Pacific Islanders speak languages of the Austronesian family. Tourism is widespread throughout the region.

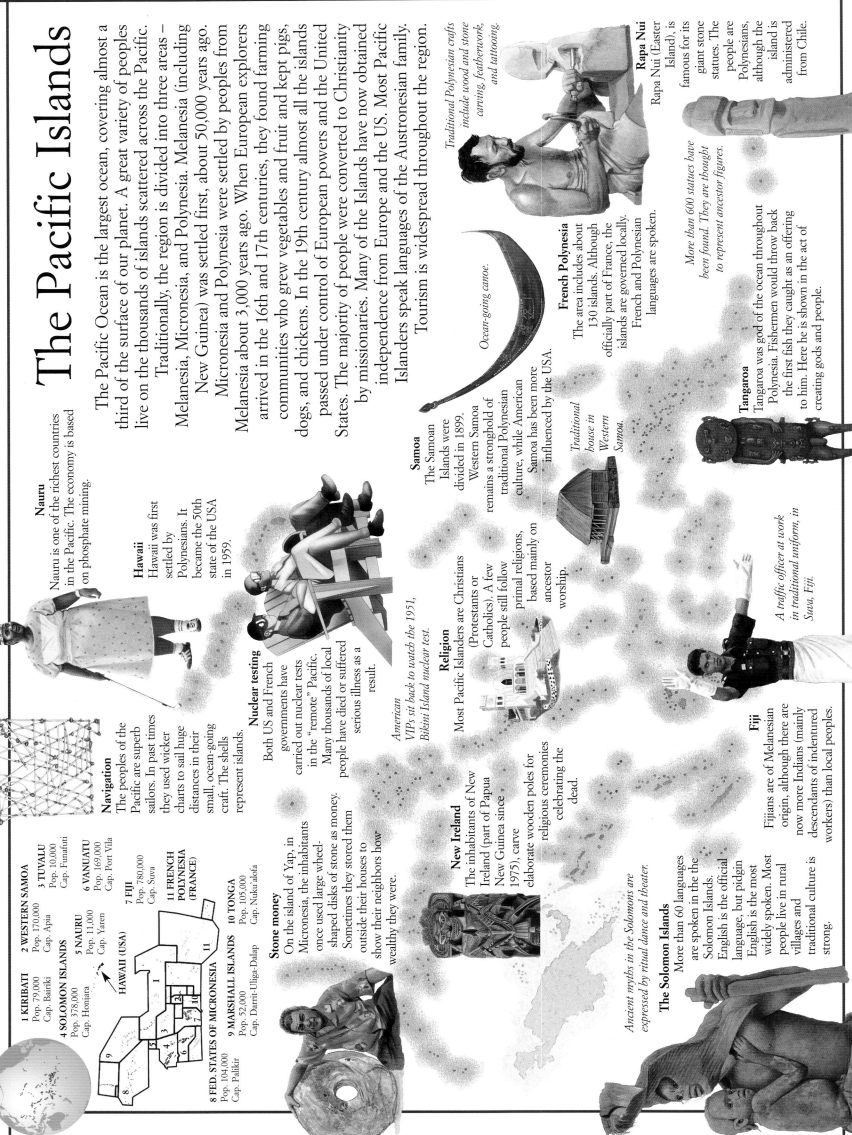

Nauru
Nauru is one of the richest countries in the Pacific. The economy is based on phosphate mining.

Hawaii
Hawaii was first settled by Polynesians. It became the 50th state of the USA in 1959.

Navigation
The peoples of the Pacific are superb sailors. In past times they used wicker charts to sail huge distances in their small, ocean-going craft. The shells represent islands.

Nuclear testing
Both US and French governments have carried out nuclear tests in the "remote" Pacific. Many thousands of local people have died or suffered serious illness as a result.

American VIPs sit back to watch the 1951, Bikini Island nuclear test.

Stone money
On the island of Yap, in Micronesia, the inhabitants once used large wheel-shaped disks of stone as money. Sometimes they stored them outside their houses to show their neighbors how wealthy they were.

New Ireland
The inhabitants of New Ireland (part of Papua New Guinea since 1975), carve elaborate wooden poles for religious ceremonies celebrating the dead.

The Solomon Islands
More than 60 languages are spoken in the the Solomon Islands. English is the official language, but pidgin English is the most widely spoken. Most people live in rural villages and traditional culture is strong.

Ancient myths in the Solomons are expressed by ritual dance and theater.

Religion
Most Pacific Islanders are Christians (Protestants or Catholics). A few people still follow primal religions, based mainly on ancestor worship.

Samoa
The Samoan Islands were divided in 1899. Western Samoa remains a stronghold of traditional Polynesian culture, while American Samoa has been more influenced by the USA.

Traditional house in Western Samoa.

Ocean-going canoe.

French Polynesia
The area includes about 130 islands. Although officially part of France, the islands are governed locally. French and Polynesian languages are spoken.

Rapa Nui
Rapa Nui (Easter Island), is famous for its giant stone statues. The people are Polynesians, although the island is administered from Chile.

More than 600 statues have been found. They are thought to represent ancestor figures.

Traditional Polynesian crafts include wood and stone carving, featherwork, and tattooing.

Tangaroa
Tangaroa was god of the ocean throughout Polynesia. Fishermen would throw back the first fish they caught as an offering to him. Here he is shown in the act of creating gods and people.

Fiji
Fijians are of Melanesian origin, although there are now more Indians (mainly descendants of indentured workers) than local peoples.

A traffic officer at work in traditional uniform, in Suva, Fiji.

---

1 KIRIBATI
Pop. 79,000
Cap. Bairiki

4 SOLOMON ISLANDS
Pop. 378,000
Cap. Honiara

2 WESTERN SAMOA
Pop. 170,000
Cap. Apia

5 NAURU
Pop. 11,000
Cap. Yaren

HAWAII (USA)

3 TUVALU
Pop. 10,000
Cap. Funafuti

6 VANUATU
Pop. 169,000
Cap. Port Vila

7 FIJI
Pop. 780,000
Cap. Suva

11 FRENCH POLYNESIA (FRANCE)

10 TONGA
Pop. 105,000
Cap. Nuku'alofa

8 FED. STATES OF MICRONESIA
Pop. 104,000
Cap. Palikir

9 MARSHALL ISLANDS
Pop. 52,000
Cap. Darrit-Uliga-Dalap

Index